The Stress Mess Solution

Executive Producer: Dan Kamerman

Editor: Mary Patrizio

Book Design: Laura Lammens

Illustrator: Don Sellers

Daniel S. Kamerman, the Sol Hurok of publishing. In today's business world, a sense of humor is as important as a commitment to quality. Dan has both.

The Stress Mess Solution

The Causes and
Cures of Stress
on the Job

by
Dr. George Stotelmyer Everly, Jr.
Dr. Daniel A. Girdano

Robert J. Brady Co. • A Prentice-Hall Company • Bowie, Maryland 20715

THE STRESS MESS SOLUTION
The Causes and Cures of Stress on the Job

Copyright © 1980 by Robert J. Brady Co., A Prentice-Hall Company. All rights reserved. No part of this publication may be reproduced or transmitted in any form or by any means, electronic or mechanical, including photocopying and recording, or by any information storage and retrieval system, without permission in writing from the publishers. For information, address Robert J. Brady Co., Bowie, Maryland 20715.

Library of Congress Cataloging in Publication Data

Everly, George Storelmyer, Jr.
 The stress mess solution.
 Includes bibliographical references and index.
 1. Job stress. I. Girdano, Daniel A., joint author. II. Title.
 HF5548.85.E93   658.3   79-14652
 ISBN 0-87619-434-X

Prentice-Hall International, Inc., London
Prentice-Hall of Australia, Pty., Ltd., Sydney
Prentice-Hall of India Private Limited, New Delhi
Prentice-Hall of Japan, Inc., Tokyo
Prentice-Hall of Southeast Asia Pte. Ltd., Singapore
Whitehall Books, Limited, Petone, New Zealand
Printed in the United States of America
80 81 82 83 84 85   10 9 8 7 6 5 4 3 2 1

ISBN: 0-87619-666-0

DEDICATION

To my wife, Gayle Schabdach Everly, whose warmth, love and support continue to allow me to grow. And to Whimpy and Paw for just being themselves.
And
to Marie, Pat and Kathy, my first family, as a way of expressing thanks for love, support, and the encouragement to never lose sight of my dreams.

Table of Contents

	Page
PART I THE NATURE OF STRESS	1
Chapter 1. The Stress Response	5
PART II SOURCES OF OCCUPATIONAL STRESS	27
Chapter 2. Work Overload	31
Chapter 3. Inactivity and Boredom at Work	39
Chapter 4. Occupational Frustration	43
Chapter 5. Occupational Change and Adaptation	49
Chapter 6. Stressful Personality Traits (The Type A Personality)	55
Chapter 7. Dietary Contributors to Stress	59
Chapter 8. Physical Environment for Work	63
PART III INTERVENTION AND MANAGEMENT TECHNIQUES	71
Chapter 9. Human Engineering	75
Chapter 10. Personality Engineering	87
Chapter 11. Roads to Relaxation (The Foundations of the Matrix Relaxation Program)	95
Chapter 12. The Matrix Relaxation Program	105
Chapter 13. Stress Reduction and Relaxation Through Physical Activity	151
Chapter 14. The Organizational Stress Audit	161
EPILOGUE	167
REFERENCES	169
INDEX	171

PART I
THE NATURE OF STRESS

On Turtles and Racehorses

Hans Selye has suggested that there are basically three types of individuals: turtles, racehorses, and those who fall in between. Turtles are individuals who are conscientious yet move along at their own pace and who resist prodding to move faster than they think they can prudently progress. Racehorses are people who aggressively gallop into work assignments, are highly achievement oriented, and consider the term "workaholic" a compliment. Of course, there are also many individuals who fall in the middle, leaning to one side or the other. This book is for all of you, no matter what type you are, because it is about work and you all have to work at some point in your life.

If you are a turtle, you may need a little coaxing to read this book, for you do take the world a little more in stride. However, we are confident it will provide you with ways of increasing your personal growth, health, job performance, and tolerance in the world of corporate racehorses! If you are a racehorse, you especially will find this book helpful, as much of the book is about you. It will show you how to optimize three important aspects of your life. It will help you increase your performance, cut your operational costs, and at the same time maintain a happy, healthy lifestyle.

"Costs of Stress High—Stress Reduction Programs Save Money"

A spokesman for the Cornell University Medical College stated that stress is "one of the most debilitating medical and social problems in the U.S. today." In addition, in the comprehensive Work in America report from HEW, on-the-job stress was indicated as a major cause of heart disease. As research on stress continues, more and more medical authorities such as these are recognizing the costliness of excessive stress.

Attempting to calculate the cost of stress to this country is a formidable task. While exact cost figures are unobtainable, it has been estimated that the cost of excessive stress to industry, and ultimately consumers, well exceeds $20 billion per year! James W. Greenwood has estimated that the **direct** costs of executive stress alone are $19.7 billion per year. Direct costs are such things as lost work days, hospitalization, outpatient care, and executive mortality.

Of greater importance is what Greenwood's figures did not attempt to estimate. The **indirect** costs of executive stress were not estimated—such things as lost creativity, lost motivation, errors in work, accidents, and slower working rates, some of which are certainly due to high stress levels. In addition the $19.7 billion figure did not include direct nor indirect costs of blue-collar stress. Furthermore there was no attempt to estimate such things as alcoholism, drug abuse, absenteeism, and even sabotage. Mental health experts feel that many of these problems are stress related. Therefore, it is clear to most industrial health professionals that the $19.7 billion estimate is just the tip of the financial iceberg.

Despite the difficulty in objectively measuring the costs of stress to business and industry, the occupational stress epidemic is perceived as severe enough to have prompted the mobilization of the capitalistic system in order to find ways of reducing debilitating stress. Companies like Hughes Aircraft, Connecticut General Insurance, and Equitable Life Assurance have made large investments in multifaceted stress reduction programs. Companies such as Adolph Coors Co., Bon Ami, and Transco have invested in meditation programs to reduce stress. All results have been very positive. PA Medical Corp. attributed a 14 percent decline in absenteeism to their stress reduction program. At Kennecott Copper stress reduction programs resulted in a 75 percent decline in sickness and accident costs. Kennecott officials estimated at least a $3 return on every $1 invested in stress reduction training. Transco officials went so far as to credit much of their company's profit rise to stress reduction programs. Results such as these have prompted companies such as AT&T, IBM, American Can, and Aetna to consider implementing such stress reduction programs for their employees.

Through effective stress reduction programs in business and industry, we may soon see corporate savings sufficient enough to be passed on to consumers—thereby creating a new lever to be used in the marketplace by competition-minded corporations. As the magazine Business Week states "stress management programs appear here to stay."

Chapter 1

The Stress Response

From the vantage point at the extreme end of the table, the 20 feet of deep rich mahogany seemed as an endless highway melting into a flat horizon disturbed only by the high-back chairs whose plush, earth-toned leather gave the appearance of stately oaks, systematically spaced and meticulously groomed so as to supply order and balance to the desolate road. But the mammoth furniture seemed as children's toys, diminished by the bookshelves towering to the 13-foot ceilings.

As Jack's eyes scanned the extensive collection, he couldn't help feeling a sense of pride, for perhaps more than anyone else in the company he had a firm working knowledge of endless facts and figures contained within their gold-embossed covers. But that is why they hired him; he really fit the description of "expert in the field." And not only was he knowledgeable, Jack was a "go-getter" as well. His life in the past five years was a testament to that.

After college he had returned home but found settling down in a small town somewhat stifling. It didn't take Jack long to master completely the job of account manager at the local mill, and at 25 years of age he was managing another CPA and two bookkeepers. During those years Jack was seen as a hard-driving, workaholic type, who was surely destined for bigger and better things. This was a reputation Jack liked and fostered at every opportunity. When this job opened up, he saw it as his big chance to move up the ladder into the world of corporate finance. The opportunity, at age 29, to manage an accounting department consisting of two accounting supervisors, four accountants, and four bookkeepers was "moving up" faster than even he had dreamed. However, he believed in his ability and knew his time would come. He often fantasized himself sitting at the head of just such a table surrounded by company executives in awe of him and grateful for his money-saving innovations.

But today was not a fantasy. Everyone had left the meeting. Jack was alone, staring across the mammoth table and trying to contain his anger, trying not to explode. He was barely controlling his overwhelming urge to take each book off its lofty shelf and smash them all into the ten portraits of the stern-faced past presidents who silently presided over every conference and provided a constant reminder that hard work was the key to success.

Jack had come into this meeting with high expectations of support and reinforcement for the job he was doing as accounting manager. Instead, what did take place was, to Jack, a devastating vote of no confidence and a condemnation of his managerial strategies. Rather than chastizing the members of his department for their lack of cooperation and carelessness on the job, the Director of Finance actually suggested that Jack was pushing his subordinates too hard. This, the Director had decided, was the reason for the significant decline in productivity from Jack's department.

Jack was furious, but he tried to control any outward expression. After all that had just taken place he couldn't afford the addition of "losing his cool" as well. However, anger is one of those stress responses which is hard to hide. Jack's conscious control allowed him to hold his tongue, but his subconscious pushed for expression. His fists were clenched, his arms flexed, his neck and shoulders taut, his back slightly hunched. Even though Jack felt controlled, his clenched teeth, squinting eyes, and wrinkled brow formed classic anger lines that were obvious signs of his internal turmoil.

Sometimes anger is somewhat contrived and is used as a conscious manipulation of others. It serves to maneuver them into worrying about you, or it loudly proclaims to everyone, "The blame is not mine! It belongs to someone else and I am not happy about it." However, if it is a real gut-level response, as Jack's seemed to be, it usually represents hurt and pain. In Jack's case he was hurt by what was said at the meeting, or more important, what he *thought* was said. Often when we feel threatened and become defensive we lose our sense of reality and begin "interpreting" what is being said. Jack was "hearing" his staff say: "We really do not have much sympathy for you. We do not care how you look to the higher ups. If you want extra work done, you do it. You're the one getting all the credit." More important, he was "hearing" them say that they did not really like him very much. Jack's feeling of anger was his attempt at striking back, a way of defending himself, of saying: "Why aren't you more like me? Why don't you have more responsibility, meet your commitments, respect authority?" As his anger continued to build, Jack's internal dialogue was interspersed with self-doubting thoughts such as "Why can't I motivate my staff? What's wrong with me!" These negative thoughts were being fueled from the "You're stupid" message Jack was hearing from his boss. Jack began the "I am a terrible person" dialogue with himself, but continued to balk at that by directing his feelings to the ones he felt were responsible for the situation, and the only way he could do that was through his anger.

Jack leaned back in his chair and tried to reconstruct the events which led to this mess; his mind would not rest until he sorted it all out. His tenure as head of the department was only a short but very full six weeks during which Jack totally dedicated his energies to transforming the accounting department into an efficient, high-performance unit. He was working seven days a week and was quick to rationalize that once he got things working smoothly he could slack off, but he had to neglect some pressing problems associated with the move to the new city. His wife, a highly qualified copy editor, gave up a good job for this move and so far was frustrated in her attempts to land a similar position here. Their older son, James, was made to repeat a grade in school and was upset that his father would not come to the school and straighten out the matter. There were dozens of other problems associated with the move as well. This was the first time Jack had ever had to fight commuter traffic. Not having had time to get into a car pool, he was driving by himself, often getting lost. It seemed as though he was forever missing his exit off the interstate. The crowds, the noise, the traffic all seemed to be a constant source of complaint and he was having a difficult time adjusting, although he could still joke about it. What seemed to trouble Jack more was the lack of communication, not only between departments, but among his own staff members. Jack's old company was smaller and, because he had been there longer, he naturally felt more in touch with the bureaucratic structure and decision-making process. The people here were friendly but the large size of the company seemed to inhibit face-to-face communication with anyone outside his own department.

Jack had been scared. Eager to prove he was the right man for the job, Jack pushed his employees to obtain higher levels of performance. On top of that, he was afraid he would fail, and the more afraid he became, the more he would push. Most of the time he felt justified in requesting that they work overtime, because he was working right alongside of them. At first, performance from the department did increase, but after several weeks error rates began to increase and absenteeism began to rise. Jack was at a loss to explain the downturn and he was worried about how this would look upstairs. He approached one of his supervisors for some insight into the problem but came away disappointed when the only suggestion made was that Jack was simply overworking his staff. Jack felt that some stress was good for the department—it worked as a catalyst or motivator to push employees to higher levels of productivity. Besides, Jack didn't ask anyone to work harder than he did. Jack began to notice a coldness and uncomfortable silence from the accountants and bookkeepers. Feeling this display of immaturity was the last straw, he requested a meeting with his bosses: the comptroller and the vice-president in charge of finance.

Jack had developed a respect for both these men and felt that their talking to the staff would serve as a motivator. That strategy backfired as their only comment was that Jack was pushing too hard. After all, this was a step into the fast-moving world of corporate high finance where his expertise with figures and programs would have plenty of opportunity to show itself. Little had he known that his job as manager of the accounting department would entail playing nursemaid to his employees. Now Jack was angry at the lack of support and professional respect his employers had shown him, but he was also angry at himself for rushing into a job without fully understanding that it involved managing people more than numbers and programs.

Jack was feeling miserable. He could not get his mind off of the ill-fated meeting. It was a certainty that he was not going to get any work done so he decided to leave work early that day. After all that he had endured, fighting rush hour traffic was adding insult to injury. It was impossible for him to get his thoughts off the meeting and he was feeling stupid for not being able to shake his feelings off. Jack thought he was made out of sterner stuff than that. He had always prided himself on his self-control and often fantasized himself standing up under fire, saving the day for everyone. He felt that he had failed himself, and his feelings were now more resentment than anger. He resented his boss, the staff members, the company structure, the extra strain of relocating and having to deal with everyone's problems while working overtime trying to get off on the right foot. He resented being put in this position. With each addition to his resentment list he would push the gas pedal just a little harder, as if the additional speed were breaking him from the bonds he felt were holding him back.

But the events of the meeting were in the past. The more important questions concerned his future. Would his position in the company be jeopardized? Could he regain the respect of his staff? He could not help worrying; he really needed to succeed at this job. He really wanted to run that department; he really cared about what he did and wanted it to be perfect. Surely they would not hold that against him. He could not face a demotion and there was no going back to the old job, not after all his talk about how limiting the small town and small company were to him. That would be a real catastrophe, being let go after only six weeks on the job. He could see himself driving a taxi, filling out endless applications; he felt the embarrassment of standing in the unemployment line.

One thing for sure, Jack knew he was not in a frame of mind to face a meeting and possible confrontation with the principal over his son's repeating the fourth grade. He could just see the arrogant little principal peering through his bifocals, pompously espousing the virtues of their big school system and trying to convince Jack that his son's education up to now had been totally inadequate. Jack began to construct his argument to the principal until he visualized a raging confrontation. Would he really punch his son's principal in the nose? After today he just might. Worse yet would be the social gathering planned for later in the evening. He was in no mood to meet new friends and try to do the usual impression number on them. Hell, tomorrow he might not even have a job! Besides, his stomach was turning over like a washing machine and his headache could be used for a TV commercial.

"Exit 42! Oh no! I was supposed to get off at Exit 39!"

At that point Jack felt totally overwhelmed and just wanted to pull off the road and scream. Everything seemed wrong; his job, his social life, his family life all seemed out of control, and his body was now really feeling the turmoil.

At several points in this story it was mentioned that Jack was "hearing" people say things they were not really saying or meaning. This tendency is at the root of Jack's stress response. Our imaginations are often our greatest stressors. Did you identify with Jack's situation? One way to tell is to stop and feel any of your own responses to this stressful story. Are your palms sweating a little? Does your heart rate feel a little faster? How are you positioning your body? Are your hands closed? Are your arms bent? Do your legs feel ready to spring you to your feet? Has your breathing changed? Take a quick look in the mirror: are your face muscles drawn? How does your stomach feel?

You will notice that almost every system of the body is involved in the stress response, but the responses of the cardiovascular, digestive, and muscular systems are the most pronounced and important to your health. These three systems most vividly represent the body's preparation to **defend** itself against a threat or to **run away** from a threat. These two actions were seen by the eminent Harvard physiologist, Walter B. Cannon, as the polar ends of the stress response continuum. They are now recognized everywhere as Cannon's famous "fight or flight" response.

The body prepares to run or fight by increasing the blood supply primarily to the heart and muscles. The heart rate increases, the blood pressure is elevated, and the adrenal glands pump adrenalin and a related hormone, noradrenalin, into the system. At the same time the digestive system slows down the absorption of food, steps up the manufacture of energy-producing substances, and spills large amounts of sugar and fats into the system to serve as immediate energy sources. The muscles become tense and begin to assume a defensive posture so as to be ready to spring into action.

When we actually fight or run, the stress is obvious; but in our socially-controlled environment, we are much too civilized to show such overt action. However, our body is not a social entity, but a psycho-physiological reactor, responding to subtle threats to our egos and our ideals. The stress debt demands a high payment in the form of our most precious resource, our health. This debt has accumulated over time. It was passed on from our distant ancestors in the form of an effective physical mechanism of dealing with stress, the fight or flight reaction. This inherent response does us little good as we now live in a "civilized" society filled with many threats, but with few means of resolution of the insuing stress.

It is important to note that much of the stress our bodies experience is not apparent as the body has a survival mechanism of temporary adaptation. Another noted stress researcher, Hans Selye, explained this adaptation in his model called the General Adaptation Syndrome, popularly known as the 3-phase G. A. S. In the first phase, the **alarm reaction**, stress is generalized and is apparent as the activity of most body systems is elevated. In the second or **resistance** phase the body "appears" to be adapting in that the stress arousal seems to be localized in one or two body systems with little or no apparent symptoms. In the third stage, known as the **exhaustion** phase, the system seems to be saturated and may break down sending the body back into a more apparent and generalized stress reaction. Exhaustion can mean death or disease. Selye points out that adaptation in this way may lead to a disease of adaptation in which the adaptation itself allows for secondary deterioration. This model may also explain why stress affects different people in different body systems. Perhaps the system which "absorbs" the stress during the resistance phase eventually becomes dysfunctional due to fatigue or becomes susceptible to invading bacteria.

Whether you have apparently experienced any of the same symptoms as Jack or not, read the next section to find out what is going on inside of Jack.

Jack's Physical Reaction

It is difficult to see most of the stress arousal which is going on in Jack's system, since only a few symptoms of stress come to the surface before pain and dysfunction signal that there is serious damage. Because we know what generally happens during stress, we can work from the symptoms Jack did demonstrate and we can put together an accurate picture of what was going on in his body. As the muscular system provides our best example of stress, let's start there.

The Effects of Stress on the Muscular System

The muscles are your only means of expression. You cannot move toward pleasure or away from danger without muscle movement. Speech, facial expression, eye movements, every mode of expression and of feeling, and every resolution of an emotion are achieved through muscle movement. No matter how hard you work to hide your feelings, the muscles usually betray you, giving to most trained observers a fairly accurate account of what you are going through. Jack showed several classic muscular responses. He clenched his teeth and frowned while at the same time he pulled his neck muscles taut. His posture was hunched over as in an attack position, punctuated by occasional clenched fists and bent arms.

To Jack, this represented only a temporary response, but it does show that he was very stressed and further shows that the muscles are an important part of his response. Continuation of Jack's present lifestyle will start to take its toll as 1) chronically tense muscles (or muscles that are contracted much of the time) complete a feedback loop and further stimulate the mind, resulting in heightened stress states, and 2) chronically tense muscles result in numerous psychosomatic disorders, including headache, backache, spasms of the esophagus and colon (the latter resulting in either diarrhea or constipation), posture problems, asthma, tightness in the throat and chest cavity, some eye problems, lockjaw, muscle tears and pulls, and perhaps rheumatoid arthritis.

A muscle is actually a mass of millions of muscle cells which have the ability to shorten when stimulated by the nerves. This shortening moves bones, skin, or some organ, and work is accomplished. Often an incomplete or partial contraction occurs, tension develops, but no work is done. It is this situation that is referred to as "muscle tension" and is linked with the disorders previously mentioned. Pain probably develops because of a lack of adequate blood supply being delivered to tissues when a partially contracted muscle closes the vessel. Pain can also develop from a chronically shortened muscle's abnormally exerting a pulling pressure on a joint, or from the tearing of fibers which can result from overexertion of a chronically shortened muscle, or just from the disruption of the proper function of an organ, which is the case with the smooth muscle disorders such as diarrhea, constipation, or spasms of the esophagus.

All muscle movements represent finely coordinated action involving an unbelievable number of commands from both the conscious and subconscious centers of the brain. Even when you "will" a movement, you only think of the action in behavioral terms. You do not direct each and every muscle; this job is done subconsciously. For example, you have just to think "pick up the pencil," not figure out how to accomplish the act. Considering this process in the context of stressful muscle tension, envision a potentially threatening situation in which you are contemplating defensive maneuvers. You think defensive, you prepare to move, you assume a defensive posture automatically. Whether the threat is real or not is unimportant. What is important is that you develop memory patterns for such activities which can be assumed without conscious thought. The muscle action for bracing, defensive posturing, or preparing for action can be completed even though the conscious mind is not actively contemplating such action. As a result, covert fears or anger can result in chronic stressful muscle tension.

While anticipation is necessary for preparation, it has been found that muscle tension develops and remains until the task is completed or the mind is diverted to a new thought process. Interestingly enough, successful completion of a task results in more rapid resolution of muscle tension than does failure at the task. Furthermore, imagination of a muscle movement or an action (for example, a defensive posture) will result in the same preparatory muscle tension as occurs when one is actually engaging in the activity. This may explain why highly anxious individuals who are often in a heightened state of expectation often exhibit elevated muscle tension. The body is very adaptive, and if muscle tension is prolonged it will adopt and create a "tone" of increased tension which feeds back to the nervous system, increasing general arousal and thus causing a general tendency to overreact. Of course, the converse is also true; that is, if the inherent rhythm is dominated by a low arousal, tranquil rhythm, one has the tendency to remain cool and collected.

The Effects of Stress on the Gastrointestinal System

Unlike the muscular system, which broadcasts its stress arousal, the gastrointestinal (GI) system hides it very well, at least from others. The owner of the stressed system gets a lot of messages. Some, like the ulcer, are very loud and clear. Several hours after the meeting Jack felt nauseated, had no appetite, and felt a burning sensation in his throat and chest area, which probably resulted from increased stomach acidity. These are not uncommon complaints of those whose GI systems seem to take the brunt of their stress arousal. You might wonder why the GI system would be involved at all, as it serves no function in the fight or flight response and logically should not be controlled by anticipatory or interpretative centers of the brain. Yet, the GI system so clearly has been recognized as part of the emotional response to stress that perception of its state of being has become part of most anxiety tests. Statements such as, "I have no appetite," "I have a gnawing feeling in the pit of my stomach," and "I feel nauseated" are the most often described physical symptoms of anxiety and emotional arousal. The formation of ulcers has even been attributed to professional decision-making.

Response to stress arousal can be measured in every structure along the digestive tract, starting with the mouth. Beginning with Pavlov's classic studies, it has been clearly demonstrated that emotional states influence the flow of saliva. Getting up before an audience to deliver a speech inevitably results in decrease in saliva. Yet, the dentist preparing to drill a tooth often turns on saliva to the point where it must be continuously removed. Emotional stimulation has also been shown to induce spastic contraction of the muscles of the esophagus, disrupting rhythmic peristalsis and making swallowing difficult and in some situations impossible.

The GI system definitely responds to emotional situations, but in a complex manner. The lining of the stomach offers a good example. In situations described as producing anger, resentment, or aggression, the stomach lining increases its secretions of hydrochloric acid and becomes engorged with blood. The membrane becomes so frail that eruptions can occur spontaneously and ulcerations can develop. On the other hand, situations described as producing fright, depression, listlessness, or feelings of being overwhelmed produce the opposite reaction—that of gastric hypofunction, in that decreasing the blood flow to the mucous glands diminishes the natural protection afforded the cells against the caustic enzymes and hydrochloric acid, and even normal levels of acid can damage the interior walls of the stomach and intestines.

14   THE STRESS MESS SOLUTION

Similar patterns have been observed in the intestines, and stress arousal has been shown to disrupt normal peristaltic rhythm. This alteration in normal peristalsis in both small and large intestines is responsible for two of the most classic stress responses: diarrhea, if movements are too fast, prohibiting normal drying through water absorption, and constipation, caused by excessive drying by prolonging transport time. Chronic constipation can further lead to more severe intestinal blockage. Blockage of the bile and pancreatic ducts, as well as inflammation of the pancreas, have also been linked with stress arousal, but more research needs to be conducted in this area.

The Effects of Stress on the Cardiovascular System

Like most people under stress, Jack was unaware that the function of his heart and circulatory systems was being so drastically altered. For a short period of time Jack was aware of his heart pounding faster and with so much intensity that he could feel it echoing throughout his body. But such palpitations are only the tip of the iceberg and are only a small indication of the potentially devastating effects of stress on the cardiovascular system.

It should be obvious that the fewer times a heart must contract, or beat, to accomplish its necessary supply functions, the more rest it will get. The heart has an inherent rhythm and, if left alone, it will beat approximately 72 times per minute. However, the heart is constantly receiving impulses from the brain directly and indirectly through the endocrine system which can alter this natural rhythm. Thus, the heart is under moment-to-moment control of various centers of the brain which are in touch with the needs of the body. A significant survival mechanism of the cardiovascular system exists in its capability to anticipate demands by increasing action of the heart before an activity actually produces a demand. Anticipation increases the activity of the system, but in our socially controlled environment our final action is often thwarted by the mind, which is conscious of sanctions against physical responses; thus the arousal is to no avail. Similarly, numerous psychological states, like the one Jack was in, increase cardiovascular activity when no action is actually required. The unknown character of most "first-time" experiences frequently elevates heart rate, as do fear, anger, anxiety, and most situations that threaten the ego. Tying this information together with that previously discussed should complete a picture that stress is a physical response, but our stressors which trigger that response are social, psychological, or symbolic, requiring no physical action. In a manner of speaking we have played a cruel trick on ourselves and have in many ways become "too civilized," overcontrolled. We do not want to be overly pessimistic about this, for it is not a hopeless problem, but you should firmly affix in your mind the roots of our stress.

Getting back to Jack's situation, it is doubtful if he or anyone else can be aware of one of the most insidious effects of stress arousal—high blood pressure, or hypertension. It has been estimated that perhaps 15 to 20 percent of the adult population suffer from hypertension, usually considered to be blood pressure above 160/95. Approximately 90 percent of the cases are **essential hypertension,** which means they are of unknown origin. Blood pressure is the pressure exerted by the blood on the blood vessel walls. Since the primary work of the heart is to overcome the pressure in the arteries to which the blood must flow, increasing blood pressure greatly increases the work of the heart and contributes to cardiovascular problems.

Like the heart, the blood vessels have an inherent tone which can be altered moment to moment by both the central nervous system and adrenal hormones adrenalin and noradrenalin. Anticipation and psychological states such as fear, anger, and anxiety will constrict the vessels, thus increasing blood pressure; higher blood pressure is a physical response to symbolic or imagined threats.

Another problem area concerning the cardiovascular system relates to the destruction of the vessels by the infusion of fatty plaques; this disorder is called **atherosclerosis.** The relationship between stress and vascular pathology appears to lie in the fact that during stress arousal, the hormones epinephrine and cortisol mobilize fats and cholesterol for use by the muscles and these circulate in the bloodstream until used or reabsorbed. Although there are many precipitating factors in the development of atherosclerosis, constantly saturating the system with unneeded fats through the stress mechanism can only exacerbate the problem. It is well known that these plaques contain cholesterol, triglycerides, and other lipids. An artery infused with such plaques will eventually lose elasticity and harden, producing the disease **arteriosclerosis** (an advanced form of atherosclerosis), which is directly responsible for over one-half million deaths annually in the United States.

When an artery in an advanced state of pathology loses its elasticity, it elevates the blood pressure, thus contributing to hypertension and pathology of the heart itself. In addition, atherosclerotic plaques, which narrow the diameter of the vessels, diminish oxygen delivery and may precipitate a myocardial infarction, or heart attack, if the coronary arteries are affected.

Looking Back on Jack's Situation

Jack's situation can be seen in graphic form in Figure 1.1.

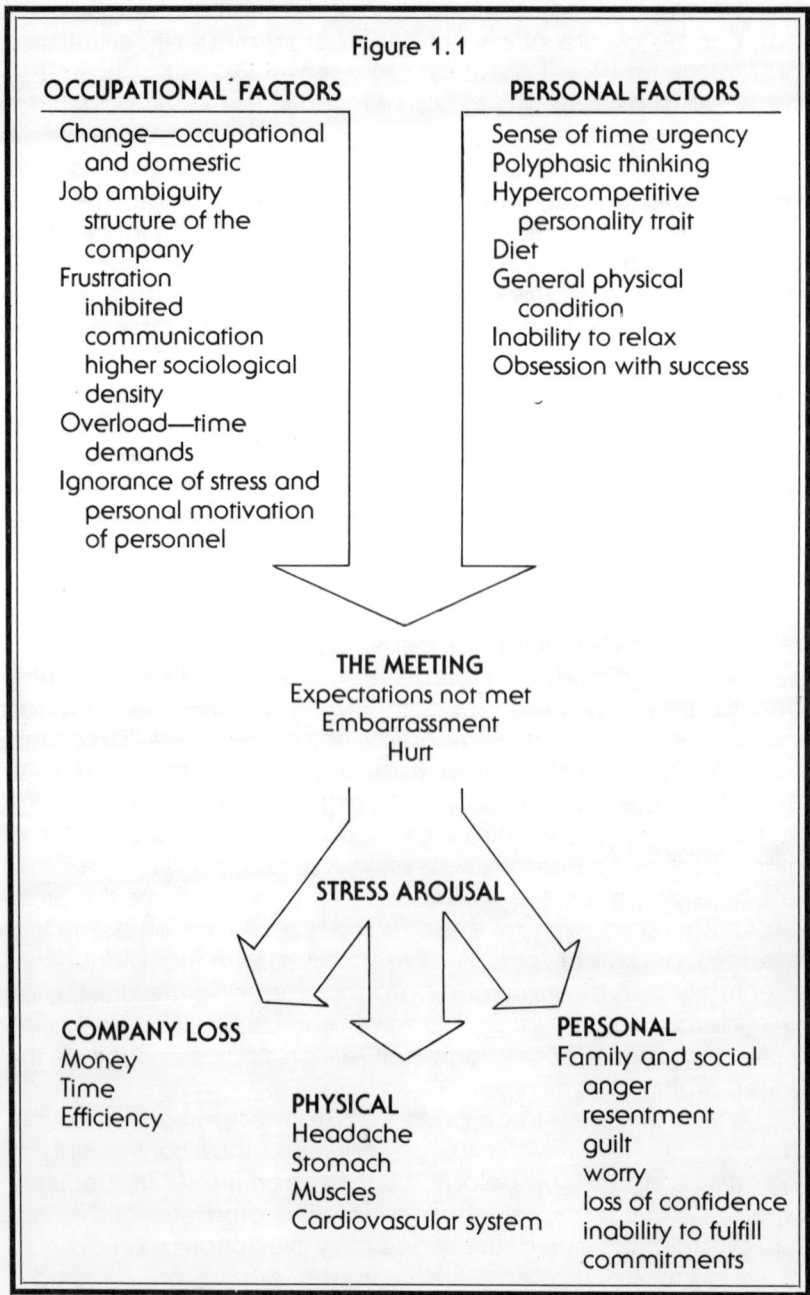

Figure 1.1

THE STRESS RESPONSE 17

From this diagram you can see the factors in Jack's life that precipitated the stressful situation. It is important to realize that this one incident is not isolated from Jack's life in general; no stressful event ever is. The event did produce a "moment" of stress. Jack's expectations were not met, he was embarrassed and hurt and he became angry. The event had some inherent stress built into it, but, by and large, it was made stressful by factors directly related to the job and by Jack's personal reaction.

Novelty and change demand adaptive energy and are always stressful. Changing jobs, changing level of responsibility, changing location are situations demanding that one adapt. Preparing to move, moving, getting settled in a new house, finding new places to shop, new schools, new bank, new barber, new friends—the list is endless. No matter what the new position demands of a person, there is plenty of adaptive energy being spent just on personal factors. But Jack had a double whammy—work overload. Whether from actual or perceived expectations, Jack felt a need to prove himself immediately, and the more insecure he felt, the more he pushed. It also became obvious that Jack had some ambiguity as to what exactly was expected of this position. He was unable or unwilling to establish an effective level of communication up or down the bureaucratic structure. Another important factor which allowed this situation to develop was Jack's basic lack of understanding of stress and motivation of employees. Noted stress researcher Hans Selye has written that stress can be a positive, creative, and motivating force, or it can be a negative, debilitating, and dangerous force. The former he calls **eustress** and the latter he calls **distress.** One important difference between eustress and distress can be explained in terms of quantity of stress as graphically represented in Figure 1.2.

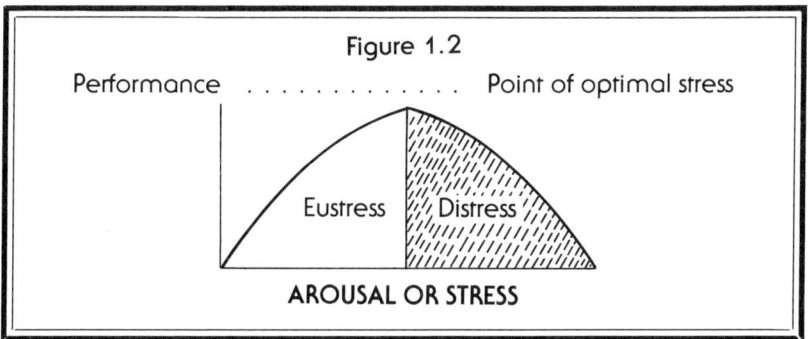

As the arousal increases, performance will also increase as you become more motivated. It is not unusual to hear people say they work better under pressure. However, if that pressure is excessive, it becomes distress . . . performance will rapidly decline and health will suffer. Jack did not understand this concept and precipitated distress among members of his staff.

Equally important to this situation were Jack's personal reactions which were in part exacerbated by his physical condition. Jack had been working long hours while at the same time trying to get his family settled in this new place. He took almost no time to relax and, while he was normally an athletic person, Jack had not engaged in any physical exercise for over a month. He was often eating on the run, picking up something at fast-food restaurants and finishing it while driving home. He was staying up late and drinking much more coffee than was normal for him.

Emotionally, Jack was beginning to wear a little thin. His recent life events, especially the time pressures, were devastating to Jack, who always worried about getting the most done in the shortest amount of time. He was naturally an efficient person with good powers of concentration and problem-solving abilities. The events of the last two months seemed to demand attention to endless detail and Jack constantly found himself focusing on two or three thoughts at once. At the same time he was becoming more frustrated over his lack of ability to concentrate and completely solve any one problem. It seemed he was more and more stopgapping and dealing with situations on the verge of being out of control.

Jack was basically competent and he felt that way most of the time, but, like many of us, he had fallen into the worry, guilt, and anger trap as a defense of his insecurities. His conscious social self told him he was well qualified for his new position, but he had some gut-level feelings of not being able to live up to everyone's expectations of him. His self-concept was that of the rising young executive, strong husband, and wise father, and that image left him very little room to express his hurts and fears. He kept his feelings to himself fearing others would think him weak, less than masculine if he expressed what he was really feeling. This, of course, represents one of the most prevalent of the self-defeating behaviors practiced in our society. Like many of us, Jack had fallen victim to the "life is tough, so I must be tough also" attitude, rationalizing his behavior as being what is necessary for success. Year by year, Jack worked harder to "become" the image of success he had pictured in his mind. This attitude went a long way to allowing this stressful situation to develop.

The Concept of Psychosomatic Illness

The event in Jack's life that we have gone to such lengths to develop was an event isolated in time, 2:00 PM, September 11, but the fact that it happened at all is a direct result of numerous factors, some as old as Jack, such as personality development, others several months old and associated with the move and the new job, and still others more immediate in the form of the structure of the company and the meeting itself. The important idea for you to understand is that what happened before the meeting was more important than what happened during it. His anger was just the tip of the stress iceberg and this incident itself now becomes just one part of Jack's total stress response which, if continued on this level, will spell trouble for his health and social functioning. It will be no surprise if Jack eventually develops a psychosomatic illness. This incident, what preceded it, and what followed represent building blocks for that illness; the incident should not be seen as an isolated event starting the day the pain or dysfunction surfaces.

There is a general misconception that illness starts when the symptoms first appear, but in most illnesses the more observable symptoms are preceded by less recognizable and less disabling symptoms which go unnoticed by the unaware. In the case of psychosomatic illnesses, the more observable symptoms are preceded by malfunctioning of an organ system, which is preceded in turn by fatigue of an organ system, prolonged physical and emotional arousal, usually in response to a social or environmental situation. The more observable symptoms become our triggers for action because we are taught to act on health matters only when we hurt or when organs no longer function properly. What precedes pain or dysfunction is physical arousal which may persist undetected for months, even years. Imagine what would have been different in Jack's life if he had heeded the early warnings of fatigue and stress. The incident would in all probability not have happened. Jack would have been able to handle the situation. Equally important, Jack's stress should serve as his early warning of future problems. This incident is a less observable symptom because most people will not link it with developing illness. That is, while aware of the arousal, most people do not link it with physical illness and, even more significant, there is a tendency to become tolerant of emotional arousal. Because of the process of adaptation, hyperarousal eventually passes as the normal state. How often have you, after finishing a prolonged project or upon starting a vacation, experienced an extreme sense of relaxation and let-down? It was only then that you realized just how tense you were; yet during that stressful time you felt normal. Often, there is a large difference between the relaxed state and your "normal" state. The lesson here is that you must develop the ability to know just how stressed you are and must learn to feel and to sense the tension you are holding captive within your body. Remember the biology experiment in which a frog is placed in water which is slowly brought to a boil. Not being able to sense the change in water temperature, he dies without ever feeling the heat. The best way for us to know how hot our life's water is is to feel the changes that are going on within our bodies, to bring into our awareness what was heretofore a less observable symptom.

Other less observable symptoms include certain attitudes, lifestyles, and personality traits which research has firmly established as being related to illness. A recurrent theme to which much importance is attached in this system for stress reduction is **lifestyle**. Evidence shows that some lifestyles clearly lead to or augment the development of psychosomatic illness. Thus, where you live, how you live, how you work and play can be determinants of health. The ability to recognize the less observable symptoms and to know when and how to intervene in the development of illness is one key to prevention. Let's take a look at some techniques.

Mapping Strategies for a Stress Reduction Program

How stressfully we react to our environment is determined, to a large extent, by our attitudes, values, personality, emotional development, and our ability to alter the influence of our environment through such factors as relaxation, diet and physical activity patterns, and the modification of lifestyle. Understanding this concept of stress makes one realize the futility of trying to deal with such a multidimensional problem with one activity or technique. Since stress reactions occur on various levels, stress management must be **holistic**, that is, must be approached from numerous and varied perspectives, simultaneously incorporating the mental, the physical, as well as spiritual, social, and environmental interactions.

The Holistic System

The Holistic System for reducing stress and tension consists of the following four sets of strategies: 1) techniques designed to minimize the frequency of stress; 2) techniques designed to allow one to become better prepared physically and emotionally to withstand excessive stress; 3) techniques designed to utilize appropriately the by-products of excessive stress arousal, and 4) techniques designed to make the organization itself less stressful.

1. Techniques designed to minimize the frequency of stress: Human and Personality Engineering.

Our environment is filled with stressors; the action or behavior of each individual or institution in the world becomes the input to other individuals. As we go about our daily activities, each individual with whom we interact, the people we live with, those in the next car, the ones we pass on the street, sit with in meeting halls, and to some extent those we see on television present some manner of stimulation. Obviously the more people, the greater the opportunity for contact. The intimacy of that contact is also of prime importance, for it is not only the behavior of others that becomes our stimulation; in addition, if we know them well enough, so do their thoughts, dreams, and unspoken expectations become our stimulation. Likewise, people and the pursuit of life create other potential stressors—from noise pollution to competition for a seat on the bus, a place on the highway, or a position with the company. Generally speaking, more people means more complexity in social as well as in institutional organization.

One of the easiest and most effective techniques of stress management is to identify stress-promoting activities and to develop a lifestyle that modifies or avoids these stressors . . . activities as simple as altering the time one gets out of bed and the route driven to work or as complex as making lifestyle decisions encompassing the choice of profession, mate, or life's goals. **Social engineering** is the technique by which an individual can willfully take command and modify his or her life. In one sense, it represents the most conscious point of intervention, but as stress management becomes a way of life, one begins unconsciously to modify one's position in relation to his/her sources of stress through the selection of a less stressful lifestyle.

Although social engineering strategies may be simple or extremely complex (based upon the nature of the stressor), one thing is definite—there are virtually unlimited strategies available to the imaginative individual. This text proposes numerous guidelines that the reader can follow to make social engineering an extremely valuable asset in the Holistic System of stress reduction.

We are a hard-working society with an industrious heritage. Half of our waking day is usually spent working, but, more than just filling our hours, work supplies much of our happiness and ego gratification. However, anything done with that intensity also has the potential to greatly influence our lives and can be a source of disappointment, frustration, and unhappiness. To most of us the stress of work supplies far more than half of our stress load. The importance of this emphasis on work is reflected in this book, which gives specific techniques to help combat the kinds of stress engendered by our work.

To a large degree, the amount of stress precipitated by our work depends upon what information is taken in and what is blocked. The way the information is perceived, evaluated, given meaning, and the way these procedures influence both mental and physical activity are important determinants of the stressfullness of the activity.

Our **attitudes** are the way we look at things, the meanings and values we assign to various events in our lives, and these, in combination with characteristic ways of behaving, or behavioral patterns, can be referred to as an individual's *personality*. The personality has the awesome capacity to transform a normally neutral aspect of one's life into a psychosocial stressor. Few events are innately stressful, but we make them stressful by the way in which we perceive them. A person may alter these stress-causing attitudes, or perceptions, by first becoming aware of the attitudinal processes and then working to alter attitude formation through the process of **personality engineering**. If personality engineering is effective, the perception of a particular life event is altered to the point where physical arousal is diminished or prevented.

2. **Techniques designed to allow you to become better prepared physically and emotionally to withstand excessive stress: Relaxation Training.**

The information being sensed from the environment is actually alerting our nervous system by two distinctly different pathways. One is conscious, voluntary, active thought processes and the other is essentially subconscious appraisal of sensory stimulation through what is called the **autonomic nervous system.**

The autonomic nervous system prepares the body for any potential action which might be needed and it does this automatically, through certain muscular, cardiovascular, and hormonal changes. However, action or responses themselves are conscious and occur only after the appropriate part of the brain perceives and evaluates the situation. Thus, the stress response, which is physical arousal, can be elicited by conscious voluntary action or by subconscious, involuntary (automatic) activation which keeps the body in a state of readiness. If the body remains in this state for long periods, the organ systems become fatigued and the result is often organ system malfunction. The constant state of readiness to respond with the fight or flight response is called **emotional reactivity.**

Relaxation training reinforced by such techniques as meditation, neuromuscular and autogenic relaxation, and biofeedback-aided relaxation helps reduce emotional reactivity. Not only does relaxation training promote voluntary control over the autonomic nervous system activities associated with arousal, it promotes a quiet sense of control which eventually influences attitudes, perception, and behavior. Relaxation training will foster interaction with your inner self and you will learn by actual feeling (visceral learning) that what you are thinking influences your body processes and that your body processes influence your thought processes. You will come to know your feelings and emotions as a part of your thinking experience. Your behavior will come more from what is within you, rather than merely be responses triggered by the people and the environment around you.

3. Techniques designed to utilize appropriately the by-products of excessive stress arousal: Physical Activity.

The primary stress response is the fight or flight response. This reaction has helped ensure our survival and continues to do so, as no amount of relaxation training can ever diminish the intensity of this innate reflex. Stress is physical, intended to make possible a physical response to a physical threat; however, any threat, physical or symbolic, can bring about this response. Once the stimulation of the event penetrates the psychological defenses, the body prepares for action. Increased hormonal secretion, cardiovascular activity, and energy supply signify a state of stress, a state of extreme readiness to act as soon as the voluntary control centers decide the form of the action, which in our social situation is often no action at all. Usually the threat is not real, but holds only symbolic significance: our lives are not in danger, only our egos. Physical action is not warranted and must be subdued, but for the body organs it is too late—what took only minutes to start will take hours to undo. The stress products are flowing through the system and will activate various organs until these by-products are reabsorbed back into storage or gradually used by the body. And while this gradual process is taking place, the body organs suffer.

The solution, very simply, is to use the physical stress arousal for its intended purpose—physical movement. In our civilized society, which does not provide for killing a saber-toothed tiger nor allow us physically to abuse our neighbor, the most efficient use of the physical arousal is physical exercise. The increased energy intended for fight or flight can be used to run or swim or ride a bike. In this way one can accelerate the dissipation of the stress products, and if the activity is vigorous enough, it can cause a rebound or overshoot after exercise into a state of deep relaxation.

One note of caution! Exercise is itself a stressor, and competition adds substantially to that arousal level; and while the stress of the exercise is usually absorbed by the exercise, the stress of competition often sets in motion thoughts and feelings which linger beyond the event and become the stimulus for prolonged emotional arousal, with the rehash of missed points, social embarrassment, and self-doubt. We often confuse recreation with relaxation—they are not necessarily the same, and for most people they are usually not the same. Recreation, while fun, can be stressful, especially if competitive. Ideally, exercise to reduce stress should be devoid of ego involvement. Though strenuous, it should be a time of peace and of the harmonious interaction of mind and body. And, in that sense, it may be the most natural of the stress reduction techniques.

4. **Techniques designed to alter the organization itself—to utilize the structure and the resources of the organization to make work less stressful: The Organizational Stress Audit (OSA).**

The OSA represents a process by which the stressor points within an organization are diagnosed and then the resources of that organization are constructively channeled to reduce employee stress. To be successful, the OSA must be delicately tailored to the idiosyncracies of each individual organization. In general, the OSA is to the organization what Human Engineering is to the individual employee. As such, it represents an effective complement to the individual employee-centered strategies mentioned in techniques 1 through 3.

Thus, the Holistic System for controlling stress in business and industry is the essence of a multidimensional approach to stress management. It combines three employee-centered strategies and one organization-centered strategy to combat stress at every level possible. The Holistic System is successful not only because it intervenes on different levels, but also because in the nature of holism the whole is greater than the sum of the parts. Intervention on **only** one level is futile. But intervention on more than one level at a time has all the advantages of a synergistic intervention approach. Intervention on **many** levels is the clearest way to success. This Holistic System has been developed over the course of 7 years of research and training conducted by the authors. These research and training programs have clearly demonstrated the effectiveness of the Holistic System in reducing excessive stress (Everly, 1979a; 1979b) (Girdano, 1977a; 1977b).

PART II
SOURCES OF OCCUPATIONAL STRESS

Introduction

No matter what form of stress you suffer from, you will better be able to manage that stress in a constructive way if you have an understanding of the things that cause your stress levels to be excessive.

To assist you in learning about the stressful aspects of your job, we have designed various self-assessment exercises within our discussions of major groups of occupational stressors. These exercises will be helpful to you in several ways: 1) they will aid you in identifying what aspects of your job cause you the most stress; 2) they will increase your ability to identify stressors which may be adversely affecting the work of those around you (peers, subordinates, etc.), and 3) each discussion will give you insight and understanding into why certain things are stressful—such insight will prove helpful in reducing stress levels.

By the end of Part II, you will have created your own personal "occupational stress profile" which can be used over and over to monitor the stressful aspects of your job. Upon developing your profile, you will quickly realize that many of the stressors in your work environment are unavoidable necessities and that others are merely good business sense taken to stressful extremes. Furthermore, some stress (eustress) is actually a powerful force which can motivate you to great achievements.

The emphasis of Part II is not to convince you of how stressful business is. Rather, it is to provide you with important information and insight about potential sources of inefficiency and strain for you and your coworkers. Such knowledge will be extremely valuable in allowing you to integrate the goals of your organization with your own strengths and weaknesses. In the end both of you, the organization and yourself, will be the winners.

After you have completed the next seven chapters, you will be ready to move on to the final portion of the text—specific techniques that you may use to develop your own program for stress management.

Chapter 2

SELF-ASSESSMENT EXERCISE 1

Directions:
   Choose from the following response options to answer the questions contained in this exercise.
   a) once a day or more
   b) more than once a week but less than once a day
   c) once a week
   d) less than once a week

During the typical course of your job, how often do you . . .

_____ 1. face important time deadlines which you have difficulty in meeting?

_____ 2. feel less competent than you think you should?

_____ 3. wish you had more support/assistance in getting your work done?

_____ 4. wish you could avoid making specific decisions?

_____ 5. feel that you've got too much responsibility considering your current resources?

_____ 6. wish you had more time in which to complete your work?

_____ 7. find yourself falling behind in your work schedule?

_____ 8. find yourself getting anxious about your work?

_____ 9. feel "overwhelmed" by your job?

_____ 10. find yourself second guessing your own decisions?

_____ 11. feel exhausted after a day's work?

_____ 12. wish your work could be less complex?

Did many of these things sound familiar? Continue reading the text to discover what these things have in common and how they may influence your work and your health.

Work Overload

Have you ever felt that you simply had too much work to do? Or perhaps you felt the work facing you was simply too difficult. Sometimes you may have found yourself in a situation where both factors were present. All of these conditions represent situations in which the job demands that have been placed upon you actually exceed your perceived ability to meet those demands. When these conditions result in mistakes on the job or contribute to ill health, we can say a condition of **work overload** exists. Overload affects you by overstimulating or overarousing your psychological and physiological mechanisms. In effect, overload is a condition in which you are bombarded with excessive job demands—excessive in that they cause you to suffer excessive stress by attempting to meet all of those demands.

There can be three types of stressful overload: 1) quantitative overload, 2) qualitative overload, and 3) a combination of both. As you read the descriptions of these forms of overload, try to identify which one you seem to suffer from the most.

Quantitative overload exists when you simply have too much work to do within a limited time. While you are technically capable of completing all of the work, the time restriction is what causes the stress reaction. This form of overload is most commonly found in the production industries and in clerical occupations.

Qualitative overload exists when you suffer a stress reaction due to the fact that the work you must complete exceeds your technical or intellectual capabilities at that time. This form of overload is encountered most often in research and development organizations as well as in many of the so-called professions—health care, law, and so on.

Finally, the **combination of quantitative and qualitative overload** is commonly encountered in administrative/management positions in all industries, in all levels of the sales industry, and in entrepreneurial endeavors.

Let us examine in greater detail the occupational conditions which seem to predispose you to overload. To do this, we have selected specific instances that may sometimes evolve into overload of each type. We shall examine

1. How time pressures may develop into quantitative overload
2. How job complexity may develop into qualitative overload
3. How decision-making may evolve into a combination of both forms of overload

Time Urgency

Our society's race against the clock has been proven to be a major source of stress. Virtually every organization imaginable exhorts some form of time pressure over its employees. It may be in the form of deadlines for work projects, deadlines for reports, sales deadlines, seasonal working limitations, or even unit production quotas as in assembly-line or other factory environments. Time urgency is the most obvious condition that fosters the development of quantitative overload, because time limitations serve to create restrictions on the quantity of work that you can reasonably complete. When you attempt to complete **more** work than is reasonable for the time restriction, a case of over-arousal will exist—your heart will pump harder and faster as you attempt to work beyond your normal work rate. In addition, you will worry about what will happen if you don't complete the work, and your heart will then work even harder. A vicious cycle is begun.

In some cases deadlines will motivate you to achieve high levels of performance. However, when the time urgency causes mistakes or contributes to ill health, a condition of quantitative overload exists. At that point time urgency becomes destructive; this condition has been referred to as the **hurry sickness.** You can perhaps recall instances when you were "racing against the clock." How did you feel? Could you feel your temples pound, or your heart racing? Take a moment and try to remember the last time you were rushing against a deadline which was unobtainable.

Medical research on the effects of time urgency upon health is most revealing. Research conducted by cardiologists Meyer Friedman and Ray Rosenman (1974) concluded that chronic time urgency appears to adversely affect the cardiovascular system. The results are typically premature heart attacks and/or high blood pressure.

Even the threat of impending quantitative overload has an adverse effect upon workers. Many managers may recall the effects of time–motion analyses upon workers. Many employees tend to demonstrate contempt and suspicion for management when time–motion analyses are undertaken. The workers resent the perception of management telling them how to "do more work in less time." In some instances such analyses have resulted in work slowdowns and sabotage if implemented from strictly an authoritarian point of view.

Time urgency is an organizational stressor that must be accepted in most cases; it appears to be a way of organizational life. However, later in the book we shall introduce ways in which individuals may reduce the harmful effects of time urgency on their minds and bodies while still meeting most organizational demands.

Job Complexity

Many people are under the impression that life is growing more and more complex. Have you ever felt that your work was becoming too complicated and that there must be an easier way? Or have you ever felt overwhelmed by the complexity of your job? If you have, then you have suffered from qualitative overload.

The most common factor contributing to qualitative overload is job complexity, which refers to the inherent difficulty of the work that must be done. The higher the complexity, the more stressful the job. The complexity of the work that you must perform can easily evolve into qualitative overload if the complexity exceeds your technical or intellectual capabilities at that time.

Job complexity is usually increased by the following factors:
1. Increase in the amount of information to be used
2. Increase in the sophistication of the information or in skills needed for the job
3. Expansion or addition of alternative job methods
4. Introduction of contingency plans

While it is true that the basic principles behind each of these four strategies will, indeed, increase the probability of your doing a better job, it is important to realize that, when excessive, each one of those four factors will also increase your stress arousal levels to the point where they actually inhibit your performance. Therefore, there is actually a point where increasing the complexity of the job no longer proves productive, but actually proves destructive. At this point you have surpassed your abilities to problem-solve and reason in a constructive way; mental fatigue and emotional and physical reactions ensue, and all of these reactions are forms of stress response.

Medical research suggests that emotional and mental fatigue, headaches, and gastrointestinal disorders are common outcomes from chronic conditions of qualitative overload.

Decision-Making

Decision-making is a source of stress that pervades all aspects of life in general. Yet it has special applicability to the world of work.

Decision-making represents a unique combination of factors which may eventually lead to the development of quantitative and qualitative overload conditions at the same time. Let us examine decision-making as a potential source of occupational stress.

Decision-making involves making a choice. Inherent in this process is evaluation, that is, determining the relative merits of one alternative over another. The stressfulness of any decision-making process will be determined largely by the following factors:

1. The relative importance of the consequences of the decision
2. The complexity of the decision
3. Sufficiency of the information available
4. The locus of the responsibility for the decision
5. The amount of time allotted for the decision-making process
6. The expectation of success

The importance of the consequences for any decision greatly contributes to the stressfulness of that decision-making process. You know, for example, that deciding what kind of car to buy is more stressful than deciding where to eat lunch. There is simply more at risk, more to be lost should your decision be a poor one.

As we discussed previously, the complexity of the decision will contribute to its stressfulness. If the decision that must be made is a complex one, involving many interwoven plans, processes, and contingencies, the decision-making process will be a stressful one. The key to the successful handling of a complex decision is being able to ascertain what is meaningful and what is superfluous information and being able to organize and synthesize that information.

While too much information can make decision-making stressful, you will find that insufficient information can lead to even greater stress. If you have ever lacked sufficient information to make a decision, you know how frustrating such circumstances can be. We have chosen to discuss this topic under overload because of the way most people react to such a condition. If you are faced with insufficient information for making a decision, your first reaction is usually to guess, or to extrapolate, the needed information. In most cases this guessing game results in a significant psychological strain as you attempt to foresee all of the potential possibilities. This strain is overload.

Another factor that surely increases the stressfulness of decision-making is the locus of responsibility, that is, who will be responsible for the decision. It is more stressful if one person is faced with singular responsibility for a decision than if that responsibility can be shared. It is interesting to observe that many executives insist upon singular responsibility. This is due to the fact that within many such systems the individual will receive full recognition for a job well done. This system is also very quick to point out consistent incompetency. The fact remains, however, that such singular decision-making processes can be highly stressful and thus may stifle creativity in some individuals; in effect the status quo may be perceived as the safest decision to make.

Time is another factor which must be considered in determining the stressfulness of any decision-making process. With only a few exceptions, we can say that the shorter the amount of time allotted for the decision-making process, the more stressful that decision process will be. One notable exception is in the case where you are given far more time than is really required. Such conditions seem to breed worry and reconsideration. In many cases you might go back and change your mind, a habit which often leads to a less effective decision.

Finally, the expectation of success figures into the stressfulness of the decision-making process. A comprehensive review of studies conducted by Jones (1977) suggests that if you fully expect to make a correct decision, your stress levels will be lower than if you are not sure. Typically, the probability of making a correct decision will be enhanced as well. However, it is important to note that if you fully expect to fail at some decision-making process your stress levels may be low also. Such a negative self-fulfilling prophecy may be used to cope with the stress involved in decision-making. For example, if you expect to fail there will be no disappointment when you do indeed fail. After all, it was expected. The only problem with this stress reduction strategy is that it greatly increases your probability of failure. Therefore, it is a destructive coping mechanism.

The amount of stress involved in the decision-making process may be expressed:

Decision-Making Stress = Importance + Complexity + Lack of Information + Responsibility + Lack of Time + Lack of Confidence

This multifaceted nature of the decision-making process explains why decision-making can result in quantitative and/or qualitative overload. How many of these factors adversely affect your day-to-day decision-making?

Summary

We have reviewed the nature of work overload as an **overstimulation** of the individual and we have also examined several of the most common precipitating conditions.

The effects of overload may be summarized here. Work overload as a stressor has been implicated in producing many of the following effects in workers at all levels:

Physiological (see Melton et al., 1971; Melton et al., 1977; Sales, 1969):
1. Increased heart rate
2. Increased blood pressure
3. Increased sweating
4. Muscular trembling or tension
5. Increased adrenalin and noradrenalin secretions
6. Increased gastrointestinal disorders

Psychological (see Levitt, 1967):
1. Lower intellectual functioning
2. Poorer verbal communications
3. Resentment of supervisory personnel
4. Suspicion of supervisory personnel
5. Anger
6. Increased emotional reactiveness
7. Confusion or anxiety

Behavioral (see Bass and Barrett, 1972; Cooper and Payne, 1978):
1. Decreased performance levels
2. Increased alcohol and drug abuse
3. Increased error rate
4. Sabotage

(Note: The motivated supervisor may attempt to recognize clusters of these signs in subordinates in an attempt to diagnose overload before it evolves into a major problem.)

Being placed in situations where you are unable to meet the demands of those situations will result in some form of overload. Such conditions are harmful to you as well as your organization.

To assess your current level of overload, refer back to Self-Assessment Exercise 1. Count the combined number of a) and b) responses that you made. If your total is 4 or more then you would appear to be a victim of some form of occupational role overload. Examine the items on which you scored high. Are they primarily sources of quantitative overload, qualitative overload, or both?

We will see later in the text that through human engineering and relaxation techniques you can effectively avoid many of the harmful effects of overload.

Chapter 3

SELF-ASSESSMENT EXERCISE 2

Directions:
    Choose from the following response options to answer the questions contained in this exercise.

        a) more than 5 hours
        b) from 2 to 5 hours
        c) less than 2 hours

In a typical eight-hour working day, approximately how many hours (excluding lunch) do you . . .

_____ 1. feel restless?
_____ 2. feel bored?
_____ 3. feel that you're overqualified to be doing the work you're doing?
_____ 4. find yourself daydreaming?
_____ 5. desire more activity?
_____ 6. have trouble staying interested in your job?
_____ 7. find yourself with nothing to do?
_____ 8. feel like you're wasting time?
_____ 9. have to search for something to do?
_____ 10. think you could be doing something more useful?

Is your day less rewarding than you thought? What effect does a boring work environment have on your job and your health? Read the following discussion to gain insight into the effects of boredom on work.

Inactivity and Boredom at Work

Have you ever noticed that some people become nervous when they don't have enough to do? Have you ever gone looking for something to work on when you didn't really have to? Inactivity and boredom on the job can cause a stress response to occur. It may manifest itself as nervousness, an inability to sit still, or a noticeable tenseness. Hans Selye categorizes this form of stress as **deprivational stress.**

If you suffer from deprivational stress on the job, it simply means that your job is failing to provide you with meaningful psychological stimulation. Two occupational settings are noted for this form of stress: the assembly line and the large bureaucracy.

Perhaps the best place to begin to look at boredom is on the assembly line. Here you will be asked to perform some highly repetitive task. After a relatively short orientation period, you will be able to perform the required task with a minimal degree of challenge to your psychological processes. Before long you will probably become bored with your task function and begin to search for stimulation of another kind—something to occupy your mind in a more meaningful manner. If you find such stimulation and it does not distract from your task performance, all will be fine. However, in some cases the thing that you choose to occupy your mind detracts from your job performance; you may make more mistakes or slow your work rate. In other cases you may be unable to occupy your mind; this is when your job satisfaction begins to decline.

The most notable of the reactions to boredom on the job is seen in the numerous cases of "assembly-line hysteria" which have been studied by the National Institute for Occupational Safety and Health (NIOSH). NIOSH was called in to investigate incidents of mass industrial outbreaks of illness. The illness seemed to consist of nausea, muscle weakness, severe headaches, and blurred vision. After reviewing several outbreaks of this mass syndrome, no organic reason for the illnesses could be discovered. It was then concluded that these were psychogenic illnesses (illnesses without organic cause). The majority of the cases seemed to occur under the following conditions: 1) boredom with the job, 2) repetitive tasks on the job, 3) lack of ability to communicate/converse between workers, and 4) low job satisfaction (Colligan and Stockton, 1978).

The industrial literature is full of examples of worker reactions to on-the-job boredom. Such things as low production efficiency, alcohol and drug abuse, and even assembly-line sabotage have been recorded, not to mention employee turnover due to the lack of job satisfaction.

Boredom and inactivity may affect white-collar workers as well. In our own consulting work with large bureaucracies we have observed the results of the boredom that overspecialization and job redundancy create. A common complaint from white-collar workers in such organizations is that there is "not enough stimulating work to do" in their job functions. Many of the agencies of the federal government appear to manifest this problem. In order to maintain their sanity, people who work under such conditions find ways of compensating for their low job satisfaction and stifled creativity. The most common compensation device we've seen is employees' working at minimally acceptable levels of job performance during the week and then expressing themselves on the weekend through their avocational pursuits. This "living for the weekend" attitude is certainly debilitating to the organization and yet can usually be traced back to the job dissatisfaction that was created by that same organization.

Summary

It is revealing to take a moment and review. You will recall that if you suffer from overload it is because you are being overstimulated by your job. If you suffer from deprivation it is because you are being understimulated by your job. You can then conclude that either extreme of the stimulation continuum can result in essentially the same result—stress. This relationship is depicted in Figure 3.1.

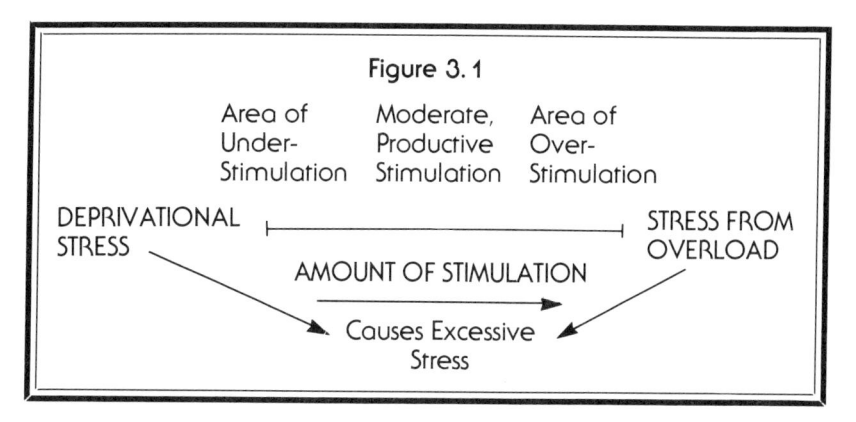

Figure 3.1

Area of Under-Stimulation | Moderate, Productive Stimulation | Area of Over-Stimulation

DEPRIVATIONAL STRESS — AMOUNT OF STIMULATION — STRESS FROM OVERLOAD

Causes Excessive Stress

Now go back and examine the questions in Self-Assessment Exercise 2. Count the combined number of a) and b) responses. If your total is 3 or more, chances are you have been a victim of deprivational stress from your job.

If your score was 3 or more, complete the following exercise:

    Step 1. Write down two ways in which you feel you compensate for your boring job.

        a) _____

        b) _____

    Step 2. Try to recall the situation in which you find yourself most bored.

By completing this simple exercise you have acquired even more valuable information about your sources of deprivational stress.

In concluding this discussion, it seems appropriate to mention the fact that some occupations may combine aspects of both overload and deprivational stressors. The two most common are police and fire occupations. These personnel find themselves in the unique position of often being bored until some catastrophic event occurs which may then result in stress from overload. In our work with these professions, we have noted the intermittent yet massive discharge of the stress response in reaction to emergency situations. Such responses have been implicated in a host of psychosomatic diseases (Lipowski, Lipsitt, and Whybrow, 1977).

Chapter 4

SELF-ASSESSMENT EXERCISE 3

Directions:
Choose from the following response options to answer the questions contained in this exercise.
- a) once a day or more
- b) more than once a week, but less than once a day
- c) once a week
- d) less than once a week

During the average course of your job, how often do you . . .

_____ 1. feel as though you're in the wrong job?

_____ 2. feel confused about exactly what your job entails?

_____ 3. feel as though your job is a "dead end street"?

_____ 4. think your skills are too specialized?

_____ 5. feel frustrated by red tape?

_____ 6. wish you could see the complete end results of your work efforts?

_____ 7. wish you had assistance in making career decisions?

_____ 8. perceive yourself as lost in bureaucracy?

_____ 9. feel frustrated by your inability to communicate within your job?

_____ 10. picture yourself as playing an insignificant role in your company's performance?

_____ 11. wish you had more guidance on the job?

_____ 12. require major clarification concerning your tasks on the job?

_____ 13. feel held back in your career or your skill development?

_____ 14. feel unsure as to how your job fits into the company as a whole?

_____ 15. feel as though you are a victim of discrimination, that is, negative assessments or actions against you on the basis of nonwork-related factors?

What do all of these factors have in common? Do many seem familiar to you? The following text discusses the implications for these factors in your job.

Occupational Frustration

Have you ever thought that your job was holding you back? Have you ever considered yourself as being lost within the organization? Have you ever wished for more of a chance to use or develop your on-the-job skills?

These are the types of thoughts that result from being frustrated on your job. Occupational stress from frustration refers to the condition that exists when your job actually **inhibits, stifles,** or **thwarts** the obtainment of expectations and/or goals that you may desire. Your body reacts adversely to the frustration of psychological desires. The result is what we know to be the stress response. If we understand occupational frustration as this sense of being inhibited, then several major sources of occupational frustration immediately come to mind.

Job Ambiguity and Role Conflict

Two of the major contributors to frustration on the job are job ambiguity and role conflict. **Job ambiguity** refers to the condition where your job description or the level of your job performance is confusing or virtually unknown to you. You may find yourself asking questions like "What should I do now?" or wondering "How did I do on the last assignment?" Job ambiguity may be caused by any of the following factors:
  1. unclear work objectives (goals)
  2. confusion surrounding responsibility
  3. unclear working procedures
  4. confusion as to what others expect of you
  5. lack of feedback, or uncertainty surrounding your job performance

Consistently, such conditions result in job dissatisfaction and significant stress levels.

Role conflict exists when your job function contains roles, duties, or responsibilities which may conflict with one another. This is most commonly found among middle managers who find themselves "caught" between the top-level management and lower-level management. Research has clearly demonstrated the middle management position to be the most stressful of the three management levels.

Role conflict may also be caused by work roles that conflict with personal, familial, or immediate societal values. Law enforcement is the profession most frequently caught in this conflict.

Once again, the result of such role conflict is job dissatisfaction and stress from frustration.

Lack of Career Development Guidance

Another potential source of stress from occupational frustration exists in the area of career development. A major study conducted in the area of job attitudes revealed that workers are demanding greater career development opportunities (Psychology Today, 1978). The following aspects of career development are considered important components of the working environment and useful in a) contributing to job satisfaction and b) preventing occupational frustration:
1. the opportunity to fully use occupational skills
2. the opportunity to develop new expanded skills
3. career counseling to facilitate career decisions

Thus, it is important for managers to realize that workers on all levels are demanding intrinsic rewards from their jobs in far greater degrees than ever before. Many large corporations and even branches of the federal government (NASA for example) have instituted formal career counseling and career development programs. The results look highly promising.

Overspecialization

In this era of highly specialized work efforts we can find another source of occupational frustration: overspecialization in job function. It has been accepted wisdom in industry that a high degree of specialization, that is, having workers become highly specific and expert in selected job areas, is a way of increasing efficiency and increasing the quality of the work. Conceptually, this is a sound procedure. However, because workers are searching for greater intrinsic rewards from their jobs, it is possible to frustrate a worker by having him/her work in a too highly fragmented or specialized job area. In our own consulting work with industry and business we are impressed with the number of employees, on all levels and in all professions, who express the desire to "see the completed fruits of the labor." Workers do not want to perceive themselves as a fragmented, insignificant cog in an immense wheel of industry. Workers want to **identify** with their companies and products—far too often overspecialization robs the worker of this reward. This problem is a serious one in assembly-line formats, and it may reach even into the professions. In a local hospital famous for its emergency "shock-trauma" department, we were surprised to find nurses expressing desires to "follow patients through recovery," not just to see them upon emergency admittance and never know how their cases progress through long-term treatment.

Bureaucracy

Another source of occupational frustration, and perhaps the most insidious source of this form of stress, is bureaucracy. Bureaucracy is a form of organizational plan. Let us take a brief look at what bureaucracy started out to be and what it is today.

The man most responsible for formalizing and advocating the utilization of bureaucracy in the twentieth century was Max Weber (1864–1920). Weber was concerned with the design of the "ideal" organizational structure based upon logic and rational thought. The four major characteristics of a bureaucracy are

1. Specialization and division of labor function.
2. The need for a set of rules governing all aspects of organizational behavior. This was to ensure uniformity and organizational stability.
3. Emotionless management. Weber felt that relationships within the organization should be typified by objectivity and be void of enthusiasm, hatred, etc. (This is a Mr. Spock approach, for Star Trek fans.)
4. A hierarchy of positions. The entire organizational structure must follow the principle of centralized hierarchy, that is, offices built upon offices, so that there exists absolute control over subordinate functions. "Bureaucracy" literally means "rule by office."

It must be understood that Weber's design was to be an ideal one. No bureaucracy yet created has lived up to the expectations of Weber. The major reason for this failure probably lies in the fact that the complexity of the human personality is simply not suited for application to the bureaucratic form of structure. Therefore, in theory bureaucracy is the most logical and efficient organizational structure possible. However, in practice bureaucracy may be the most counterproductive form of organized work effort.

Reviewing bureaucracy as an organizational entity, Gouldner (1954) and Bennis (1966) have pointed out the most common criticisms of that form of organization as it actually exists in practice today. Among them are

1. Frustration of personal and professional development
2. The fostering of mediocrity on the job
3. The reinforcement of the establishment of complex rules (red tape)

4. Stifled communication due in part to excessive paperwork (more red tape)
5. Impersonality in supervisory practices
6. Arbitrary rules virtually impossible to rescind
7. Stifled creativity

Victor Thompson (1961) summarizes what he terms "bureaupathology" as a condition where

> Employees who seem to be interested in nothing but a minimal performance of their own little office routines are numerous . . . , and impersonal treatment of clients and associates that approaches the coldness of absolute zero is not, sadly, uncommon. (p. 23)

Stifled Communications

The term **organizational communication** refers to the patterns and networks along which communications flow through an organization. Stifled organizational communication has been found to be the single most prevalent source of frustration in organizations today. Do you find yourself feeling isolated in your job, or relying on information that comes too late or not at all? Have you ever had a conversation with someone and walked away asking yourself what that person had really said? These are common communication problems. Proper planning and organizing functions depend upon effective communication. Ideally, communications flow up, from subordinates to superiors, and horizontally, from department to department, as well as in the traditional downward direction, from superiors to subordinates. In many cases organizations frustrate employees by keeping open only the downward channels. Typically, the last channel to be maintained is the upward channel. This is not only frustrating, but a gross waste of human resources. Efficient organizational communication is perceived as so important that specialties in organizational communication are being born. Special university graduate programs are even offered in this area. Efficient communication can be a powerful source for stress reduction and increased performance on the job. Unfortunately it is often overlooked or just "assumed" to be working well.

Discrimination

Our final remarks on sources of occupational frustration are directed to what is an emotional issue for many: discrimination in hiring, pay, and promotional policies. Discrimination exists at work when these policies are determined on the basis of non-work-related factors. Discrimination has long been known to be correlated with feelings of intense frustration and anger. The **Psychology Today** study described earlier found occupational discrimination a major concern of the working middle class. This topic is of special interest in today's job market because the discrimination that plagued the nonwhites and females in the work force is being replaced to some degree by the so-called reverse discrimination, wherein nonwhites and females are being looked upon favorably for jobs and promotions on the basis of race and sex. Discrimination of any type is harmful to the organization and person by leading to job dissatisfaction, anger, resentment, and a sense of hopeless depression or a "what's the use of trying to do a good job?" attitude.

Summary

Return to Self-Assessment Exercise 3 and count the combined number of a) and b) responses. If your total is 4 or more, chances are you are suffering from a form of stress from organizational frustration. It is relevant at this point to note that the harmful psychological and physiological effects of stress from organizational frustration are relatively short-lived, typically lasting less than a year. At that point most individuals who are vulnerable to such distress may leave the organization; or, they will adjust to the situation by alienating their working life from their home/avocational life (the "living for the weekend" mentality that we discussed earlier). Work then typically becomes viewed as a necessary evil in order to maintain the avocational interests. Job satisfaction is virtually nonexistent, except on pay day, and job performance is sustained on the most minimal of levels. Part III of this text discusses how you can maintain your performance levels and health in the face of occupational frustration. Recommendations for altering the organizational sources of frustration are discussed in Chapter 14. In the meantime, analyze what the sources of your frustration are:

Items 2, 11, and 12 indicate job ambiguity.
Items 3, 7, and 13 indicate lack of career guidance.
Items 4, 6, 10, and 14 indicate overspecialization.
Items 5 and 8 indicate the bureaucratic influence.
Item 9 indicates a lack of communication.
Item 15 indicates discrimination.

Chapter 5

SELF-ASSESSMENT EXERCISE 4

Directions:
  Place a check next to each of the situations described below that you have experienced within the last 12 months.

  _____ Major change in your job function
  _____ Restructuring of your organization or department
  _____ Retirement
  _____ Acquisition of a new supervisor(s)
  _____ Acquisition of new colleagues with whom you work
  _____ Any change in working procedures
  _____ Any change in administrative policy
  _____ Requirement that you develop new skills (retraining)
  _____ Any change in your work location
  _____ Pay raise (increase of 15 percent or more)
  _____ Decrease in pay of any amount
  _____ Increase in your responsibility at work
  _____ Any change in the amount of authority that you have
  _____ Any change in the amount of autonomy that you have
  _____ Any change in the number of hours that you work a week (15 percent change per week for a period of one month or more)
  _____ Change in the time of day (shift) that you work

How much change have you encountered in the last 12 months? Has it been stimulating or overburdening? This chapter may provide you with some startling information about change.

Occupational Change and Adaptation

Change within an organization is a necessary and vital component of growth and continued productivity; it can also be a source of stress for many employees.

Change is stressful because it disrupts the psychological and physiological rhythms that accompany all human behavior. The most vital fact to grasp is that change is a disruption, requiring you to expand psychological and physiological energies in order for you to adapt to a new situation. This is true regardless of whether the change is a good change or a bad change. The noted stress researcher Hans Selye summarizes this point by stating that the expenditure of "adaptive energy," in an attempt to adjust, is what makes change stressful. Change becomes harmful at that point where you deplete your adaptive energy. The end result is psychological or physiological breakdown—illness. There have been numerous research efforts documenting this phenomenon (see Selye, 1976; Gunderson and Rahe, 1974).

There are numerous sources of **adaptive stress** (stress due to change) within the organizational world. Some of the more common ones are described for you below.

Technological Change

Business and industry are continually becoming more dependent upon technology. Space-age technology has contributed to the increased efficiency of all work functions, from production to clerical processes to high-level managerial decisions. Computers appear to be the key to a successful business enterprise. However, with this expanding role for technology in business and industry comes the impact that such technological change has upon the workers. Even though technology is a very positive force in the working world, it still requires role changes for those who are affected by it. Such changes require adaptation.

Can you think of one way in which technology has required adaptation for you or your company? It shouldn't be hard. How often does technology force a change followed by some necessary adaptation? Alvin Toffler's book **Future Shock** is an excellent essay on the stressful implication of technological change. He concludes that change solely for the sake of change is harmful. Furthermore, when change is indicated, such change must be integrated into the system so as to minimize the harmful impact upon the people who must cope with the change.

Relocation

Another common source of adaptive stress is relocation, both vocational and residential. When you are forced to relocate, a great deal of stress generally follows. Even if the relocation is in conjunction with a raise and promotion, there will still be adjustment needed to cope with the changing environment. The following factors intensify your stress from relocation:
1. All of the complexities of physically moving possessions from one location to another
2. In many cases the severing of interpersonal relationships
3. The formation of new interpersonal relationships
4. In some cases, the necessity of adjusting to new cultural and/or socioeconomic conditions

All of these factors are compounded if you must relocate residence and work setting simultaneously.

For many individuals change is exhilarating. Certainly negative changes will be more stressful than will positive changes because of the psychological impact of an undesirable change. However, the point will again be emphasized: change, whether good or bad, requires the expenditure of adaptive energy and therefore is stressful. So even positive changes should be carefully considered during periods of high stress, unless of course that change removes you from your stressors.

Promotion

Promotion is another source of adaptive stress. The stressfulness of being promoted is considered by most as a small price to pay for the rewards of the promotion. Take a moment and consider the impact of the following factors which generally accompany a promotion, in addition to the obvious rewards:
1. Significant changes in job function
2. Increased responsibility for people, production, and money
3. Changes in social role which may accompany the promotion (Have you ever noticed that with some promotions come certain "social obligations" which cause intense social and even financial stress?)

Inherent in each of these factors is a considerable amount of adaptation for most individuals. Even if these factors are all positive for you, they take some getting used to.

Reorganization

Another consideration in sources of adaptive stress comes from departmental or organizational restructuring. This often happens when a new administration takes over. While such major reorganization happens rarely, it can be a major source of adaptive stress. Feelings of insecurity, anticipation, and apprehension usually dominate the minds of those affected by reorganization. If you are ever in such a reorganization, the first thing on your mind will probably be job security. After that has been successfully dealt with, your next question will typically be, "How do I fit into this new arrangement?" During such uncertain periods your work will probably fall off, or you may stress yourself through overload in an attempt to demonstrate your worth to the new management. In either case, it behooves you as well as the new management to be aware of and quickly resolve these questions of job security following reorganization.

Time Change and Biorhythms

If you must rotate work shifts you don't need this book to tell you that it is stressful, requiring significant adaptation. Even changes in time zones during travel is stressful.

To better understand how changes in working times can be stressful, we need to turn to the concept of biorhythms. The term "biorhythm" refers to naturally recurring cycles of biological activities. There are three major categories of biological rhythms:

Ultradian rhythms are rhythmic biological cycles that occur in periods lasting less than 24 hours. The most common example of an ultradian rhythm is dreaming (REM sleep). Researchers have long known that we dream every 90 to 100 minutes during normal sleep.

Circadian rhythms are biological rhythms that occur approximately in 24-hour cycles. The most noted example of such activity is the rhythmic secretion of the adrenal hormones (catecholamines). Catecholamine secretion is low in the morning and rises as the day progresses, thus accounting for mood and temperament fluctuations during the day.

Infradian rhythms are the rhythms that have gained the most popularity recently. These are the cycles typically associated with the term "biorhythm." There appear to be three main infradian rhythms: 1) a 23-day physical cycle which influences coordination and strength; 2) a 28-day emotional cycle which influences emotional responses and moods; and 3) a 33-day intellectual cycle which influences complex thought, creativity, and problem-solving.

When any of these natural rhythmic processes are disturbed or thrown out of balance, the body undergoes an adaptive stress response as it attempts to restore necessary biological rhythm and balance (called **homeostasis**).

The two most common examples of how stress affects the body when your natural biological rhythms have been disturbed are jet lag and shiftwork fatigue.

In recent years jet travelers who cross time zones have been reporting symptoms of headache, gastrointestinal problems, blurred vision, and, in females, menstrual difficulties. These collective symptoms have come to be known as the "jet lag syndrome." It most commonly affects transcontinental and transoceanic travelers. This problem could prove costly for business executives who must conduct high-level business affairs while suffering from such jet lag. This syndrome has also been found to be a major problem for the pilots and airline crews who make such flights frequently.

The other common source of biorhythm disturbance is found in frequent shiftwork changes. Workers who must alternate shifts report many of the same symptoms as are found in jet lag. The most severe symptoms occur when changing to or changing from the 11 PM to 7 AM shift. Workers who must rotate shifts have been found to suffer from more illnesses than nonrotating workers. Respiratory illnesses, gastrointestinal illnesses, and fatigue are the most common problems reported. Some workers can adapt to the time change in about a week, most workers require three weeks, and some never properly adjust to the alterations in their biorhythmic activities.

Retirement

The last major source of adaptive stress that we shall consider is the stress associated with the adjustment to retirement. It's not hard to understand why retirement is stressful for many employees. An employee may have spent most of his/her adult life working. For many workers the association between self-esteem and job is so great that they no longer view themselves as a composite of hobbies, family, special groups, **and** job, but identify themselves solely with their job. Statements like "I **am** an engineer," rather than "I am **employed** as an engineer," foster employees' tendency to replace their identity in terms of broad personal characteristics with job-related characteristics and roles. Thus, when

workers retire, particularly if they are forced to retire from a very rewarding job, the results are typically among the following:
1. Depression
2. A sense of worthlessness and loss of self-esteem
3. Decreased appetite
4. Loss of motivation in general
5. Increased cardiovascular complaints
6. Decreased sexual drive

More important, however, the U.S. Bureau of Labor Statistics reports data which suggest that those workers who are forceably retired will survive, on the average, only 30 to 40 months after their retirement.

Other factors which increase the stressfulness of retirement are
1. A great number of years at the same job
2. Lack of interests outside the job, e.g., family, hobbies, social involvement
3. A high affiliation held with the job
4. Lack of preparation for retirement, e.g., retirement counseling or just informal mental preparation
5. Lack of alternative sources of income
6. Lack of alternative sources of ego gratification (self-esteem)
7. Knowing others who have retired and encountered difficulties adjusting

Summary

In considering occupational change as a source of stress, the most important fact to keep in mind is that change forces you to expend psychological and physiological energy in an attempt to restore balance (homeostasis). The longer it takes you to adjust to the change (restore homeostasis) the greater the stress. Finally, keep in mind that while positive changes are more desirable than negative changes, even the positive changes will to some degree produce a stress response, which may act as sufficient motivation for you to consider the relaxation exercises we later describe. Similarly, in some situations it may be advisable to postpone change of any type, if it is possible. We are not saying avoid change; rather, simply be aware that change can be stressful and act accordingly.

Turn back to Exercise 4. Each of these items involves adaptation necessitated by change in your working environment. If you have checked any 4 of those items, your body and mind have been forced to undergo significant adaptation. You may consider any procedures discussed later in this book to help you adapt.

Chapter 6

SELF-ASSESSMENT EXERCISE 5

Directions:
   Choose from the following response options to answer the questions contained in this exercise.
   a) Almost always true
   b) Usually true
   c) Seldom true
   d) Never true

Answer each question as is **generally** true for you

_____ 1. I don't like to wait for other people to complete their work before I can proceed with my own.

_____ 2. I hate to wait in most lines.

_____ 3. People tell me that I tend to get irritated too easily.

_____ 4. Whenever possible I try to make activities competitive.

_____ 5. I have a tendency to rush into work that needs to be done before knowing the procedure I will use to complete the job.

_____ 6. Even when I go on vacation, I usually take some work along.

_____ 7. When I make a mistake, it is usually due to the fact that I've rushed into the job before completely planning it through.

_____ 8. I feel guilty for taking time off from work.

_____ 9. People tell me I have a bad temper when it comes to competitive situations.

_____ 10. I tend to lose my temper when I'm under a lot of pressure at work.

_____ 11. Whenever possible, I will attempt to complete two or more tasks at once.

_____ 12. I tend to race against the clock.

_____ 13. I have no patience for lateness.

_____ 14. I catch myself rushing when there is no need.

How do you feel about the answers you've just given? Read the following text and see if your impressions change.

Stressful Personality Traits
(The Type A Personality)

When an individual suffers from excessively high stress, there is often a tendency to blame it on other people or on diverse sociological factors. This tendency to avoid ultimate responsibility for your own stress is a **maladaptive coping mechanism.** It is a coping mechanism because it allows you to continue to live a stressful life—after all, "it's not your fault." It is maladaptive because you are avoiding ultimate responsibility for something that **is** within your control and it stifles the tendency for you then to assume responsibility for managing your stress. Being aware of this psychological game that many people undertake, you can imagine the typical reaction when we suggest that one's personality can actually make one's own life stressful. Can your personality actually contribute to excessive stress?

To answer that question, we will begin by defining what your personality is. Your personality consists of the sum total of all of the values, attitudes, and behavior patterns that are characteristically yours.

The fact is that certain personality traits do, indeed, cause or at least exacerbate stressful reactions. Medical researchers have uncovered four major personality traits which are most implicated in causing stress in the world of work:

1. **An intense sense of time urgency.** This trait is characterized by a tendency to race against the clock even when there is little reason to. It is almost as if there is a need to hurry for hurry's sake alone, and this tendency has been appropriately called the "hurry sickness."
2. **Inappropriate aggression and hostility.** This personality trait reveals itself in the person who is excessively competitive. This person cannot do anything "for fun." This inappropriately aggressive behavior easily evolves into frequent displays of hostility, usually at the slightest provocation or frustration.
3. **Polyphasic behavior.** Polyphasic behavior refers to the tendency to undertake two or more tasks simultaneously at inappropriate times. The results are usually wasted time due to an inability to complete the tasks.
4. **Goal directedness without proper planning.** This final tendency refers to the tendency of an individual to rush into work without really knowing **how** to accomplish the desired result. The outcome is usually incompleted work or error-laden work, thus actual wasted time, energy, and money.

Singularly any one of these four personality traits will result in high stress levels, even though they probably evolved out of what was once reasonable business behavior—time consciousness, high motivation, the desire to do more than one thing at a time, and being a "go-getter."

Collectively these personality traits are called the **Type A Personality**; sometimes they are referred to as the **coronary-prone personality** because of their high correlation to premature heart disease. This personality constellation was originally discovered by two cardiologists. During the course of treating their patients, cardiologists Myer Friedman and Ray Rosenman began to recognize a similar, recurrent pattern of personality in their patients who suffered from premature coronary heart disease (CHD). These patients seemed to be obsessed with time urgency, work, and achievement motives.

These cardiologists then undertook research efforts to substantiate their clinical intuitions that these patients possessed a common personality that predisposed them to CHD (see Friedman and Rosenman, 1974, for a description of this process). The results revealed basically the four personality traits described earlier as being the common coronary-prone traits.

After they identified the components of the Type A Personality, they went on to test the medical implications in a wider sampling. Their research supported the original proposition that Type A behavior did predispose many individuals to the development of CHD. A two-year study of 3,411 men between the ages of 39 and 59 revealed that of those within the 39 to 49 age group who developed CHD, 85 percent were originally diagnosed as Type A.

Apparently, the collective behaviors known now as Type A strain the cardiovascular system more than other physiologic systems. Studies have shown, for example, that Type A individuals respond to social stressors with significantly higher 1) systolic blood pressure, 2) heart rate, and 3) heart rate variability, when compared to non-Type A's. Type A's showed no greater galvanic skin response than did non-Type A's, however (Dembroski et al., 1977). Galvanic skin response is a measure of skin moisture during stress.

It is common for American industry actually to breed Type A's, that is, we learn to be Type A just as we learn any other personality trait. Many young executives fall into the Type A trap because they misinterpret these behaviors as being the ones that will lead to success in the business world. We have suggested how simple this misinterpretation becomes due to the fact that **under proper conditions** time urgency, aggression, polyphasic behavior, and goal-directedness could be very productive behaviors. Yet, the Type A lacks the ability to discern the appropriateness of these behaviors and behaves this way the majority of the time, in virtually all aspects of his/her life. Of the four Type A traits, however, hostility appears to be the most predictive of premature coronary heart disease.

The Type A is not only harmful to him/herself, but harmful to the company as well. Type A's can cause direct costs such as medical payments and lost time and productivity. More insidiously, however, the Type A worker often causes stress for those other non-Type A workers with whom he/she comes in contact. Haven't you ever watched someone who made you nervous simply by your observing their hurried actions? Similarly, since Type A behavior is learned, it could be somewhat contagious for some employees.

Summary

All in all, Type A behavior appears to be the Puritan Ethic run wild and distorted to the point of being dysfunctional. It represents a very difficult problem to deal with because personality is the hardest of human variables to alter within the domain of the behavioral sciences. Do you know any Type A's? Are you Type A? Turn back to Self-Assessment Exercise 5. Responses of a) or b) indicate a high score for any item. Did you score high on any of the four stressful personality traits?

Items 1, 2, 8, 12, 13, and 14 correspond to time urgency.
Items 3, 4, 9, and 10 correspond to competitiveness/hostility.
Items 6 and 11 correspond to polyphasic behavior.
Items 5 and 7 correspond to a lack of planning.

Now go back and add up the total number of a) and b) responses that you made to this exercise. If your total is 5 or greater, you possess at least a basic component of the Type A Personality. How many of the Type A traits do you have?

Later in this book we will suggest to you various methods that you may employ to turn your Type A traits back into productive working behaviors. We call such methods "Personality Engineering."

Chapter 7

SELF-ASSESSMENT EXERCISE 6

Directions:
  Place a check next to each of the situations described below that is usually true for you.

  _____ I usually eat something high in **sugar** each day (for example, candy, pie, ice cream, or cake).

  _____ I usually drink three or more cups of **coffee** or **tea** in the morning.

  _____ I usually drink three or more cups of **coffee** or **tea** with lunch.

  _____ People tell me that I use too much **salt** or salty foods.

  _____ I usually add three or more shakes of **salt** to each of my meals.

  _____ I usually drink three or more cups of **coffee** or **tea** during or just after dinner.

This chapter discusses the role of diet in your job and your health.

Dietary Contributors to Stress

Are you eating yourself into unnecessary stress? An often overlooked aspect of your environment which possesses significant potential to increase your stress level is your diet. Research has clearly demonstrated that certain dietary habits can actually increase the amount of stress in your life by 1) chemically triggering the discharge of the stress response in your body, and/or 2) making you more anxious and irritable so that you are more likely to become distressed by things in your environment that normally wouldn't upset you. Let us examine the mechanisms behind such dietary contributions to the stress response.

Stimulants

Did you ever consider what coffee (**Coffea arabica**), tea (**Camellia thea**), cola beverages, and chocolate have in common? They all contain caffeine, a chemical which belongs to the xanthine group. Xanthines are powerful, amphetamine-like stimulants. The consumption of caffeine leads to an arousal of your body's sympathetic nervous system, a part of the autonomic nervous system which triggers "speed-like" effects characterized by increased heart action, increased blood pressure, anxiousness, and most of the other responses that we know to be components of the stress response.

How much caffeine is too much? Research studies disagree on an exact amount, and certainly body weight will influence the effects of caffeine. However, most authorities suggest that consumption in excess of 250 to 300 mg of the xanthine stimulants within an hour or so will trigger a significant stress response. Coffee contains about 108 mg of caffeine per 6-ounce serving. Tea, as it is commonly brewed, has only about 90 mg of stimulants. Furthermore, tea does not irritate the stomach lining as does coffee. Leading cola beverages contain about 60 mg of caffeine per 12-ounce serving and chocolate contains about 20 mg per 1-ounce bar. How badly are you stressing yourself with these foods? Calculate how much caffeine you consume during a two-hour period. Does it exceed 300 mg? If so, chances are you're making yourself more anxious, uptight, and generally hyperexcitable than you need be—this in addition to the strictly physiological response that you've triggered.

At this point we should mention that nicotine found in tobacco is also a powerful stimulant. However exact quantities required to initiate a stress response are highly variable.

Vitamin Deficiency

Vitamin deficiency is another factor that has been implicated in increasing stress levels. Vitamins of the B complex are necessary to maintain the integrity of the central nervous system and thus to help keep you calm and relaxed. When your body depletes its supply of B vitamins, you begin to get fatigued and irritable and may have numerous anxiety spells.

One way that you will deplete your own supply of certain B vitamins is through the stress response itself. One of the major constituents of the stress response is the activity of the adrenal hormones. Vitamins B_5, choline, and C help make up the adrenal hormones; therefore, under chronic stress, you use up these vitamins at a far greater than normal rate. Vitamins B_1, B_2, and niacin are also used up at greater rates during the stress response owing to the hypermetabolic conditions that exist.

Another way to deplete your B vitamins is through the consumption of refined sugar. Harold Rosenberg (1974) discusses the role that refined sugars may play in B-complex depletion. Besides their other functions in the body, B vitamins are needed for the metabolism of carbohydrates (of which sugar is one). However, through refinement, the B vitamins in sugar are destroyed. Therefore, in order to be metabolized (used for energy), sugar must "rob" your body of existing B vitamins. This process depletes your B vitamins and increases your chances of acquiring B-vitamin deficiency along with its stress-related symptoms of fatigue and irritability.

It is necessary to state at this point that B vitamin deficiency is rare from any single cause, but may be a cumulative result of these factors and others that may be concomitant with chronic stress.

Refined sugars may be of even greater significance to the development of ill health than we first hypothesized. In the August 1978 issue of **Prevention**, Sheldon Reiser of the USDA implicated refined sugars in the development of late-onset diabetes, high blood pressure, and malnutrition. The average American's diet consists of 20 to 25 percent refined sugar. You could easily cut that level in half and still receive enough quick energy from your diet.

Salt

The final contributor to stress from a dietary perspective is salt—sodium chloride (NaCl). Excessive consumption of salt leads to increased blood pressure and has even been implicated in anxiety and irritability. The basic mechanism through which these things are brought on is through water retention. Sodium is the most osmotically active substance in the human body. This means that sodium increases your body's tendency to retain and store fluids. When your body retains excessive fluid, two things generally occur. First, blood pressure is increased through the vasoconstrictive properties of the tissue edema (swelling). Second, the edema that occurs, if great enough, may lead to a condition of hyperexcitability of nerve cells. This second condition leads to increased anxiety and nervousness.

How much is too much salt? The average American consumes 6,000 to 8,000 mg of salt per day. The active individual needs only around 1,000 to 2,000 mg per day. It is easy to see why we exceed our dietary needs when you realize that an average shake from a salt shaker yields about 100 mg—and this amount is in addition to the naturally occurring or additive quantity of salt that is in food before we even receive it.

Summary

In summary, we see that your diet can greatly affect your level of stress by actually stimulating a stress response, or by making you less resistant to the stressors that you encounter every day.

Refer back to Self-Assessment Exercise 6 and count up the number of items that you've checked. If your total is 2 or greater, chances are that your diet is contributing to your stress levels. Go back and see if there are any consistent "problem foods" in your diet or problem eating patterns. Awareness is the first step in remedying such problems. Later in this book we discuss some rather obvious ways of avoiding stress through the manipulation of your diet. We call these strategies "Nutritional Engineering."

Chapter 8

Physical Environment for Work

The final source of occupational stress that we shall examine is the physical surroundings in which you work. While there have been many aspects of the work environment which have been documented as contributing to decreased performance levels and ill health, we shall examine only those factors which have proven deleterious because of their role in facilitating the discharge of the stress response. We shall examine noise, lighting, temperature, and physical posture.

Noise

Noise as a source of stress represents a rather unique variable. It can prove stressful because of its psychological characteristics, that is, by being unwanted or distracting. It can also prove stressful simply because of its physical characteristics, that is, volume and/or frequency. Therefore, noise as a stressor has a psychological as well as a strong physiological component to mediate its overall effects on human behavior.

Perhaps the best place to begin our discussion of noise is with a few basic definitions. **Noise** is sound. **Sound** is an integration of vibrations, or mechanical waves. The **strength** (sometimes considered as intensity or loudness) of sound is measured on the basis of pressure gradients called **decibels** (dB). Zero dB represents 20 micronewtons per square meter. The decibel scale is a **logarithmic** scale; that means it is based upon powers of ten. This fact explains why an increase from 0 to 10 dB (increase of 10 dB) represents an increase of 10 times and an increase from 10 to 20 dB (increase of 10 dB) represents an increase 100 times as intense. Thus, the sound intensity multiplies by ten with every 10 dB increase. The **frequency** (or tonal quality) of sound is measured in cycles per second, sometimes called **Hertz** (Hz). Human hearing ranges from 0 to beyond 150 dB (intense pain) and 20 to 20,000 Hz.

It was suggested earlier that noise can be stressful simply because of its psychological characteristics. If any sound is annoying or otherwise unwanted, it will be stressful—no matter how low the dB level. For example, under most conditions a 35-dB noise would cause little response. However, if you were doing highly detailed work which required intense concentration, even 25 dB could be distracting and therefore stressful. Variability within a noise also increases stress. Intermittent or sporadic noises are psychologically more disturbing than are constant or predictable noises. Therefore an airconditioner or fan can actually produce a very relaxing effect due to the steady invariant rate of sound production.

The physical characteristics of noise (intensity and frequency) are the points most often mentioned in discussions of noise as a stressor.

Let us examine first the effects of intensity alone. Sound levels above 35 to 40 dB will typically awaken a sleeping person. Sound levels in excess of 55 dB are sufficient to make normal conversation difficult. Of greater biological significance are dB levels in excess of 65 to 70 dB. Evidence exists to suggest that at this level there is increased sympathetic nervous system arousal characteristic of a stress response. The major component of this response is increased adrenal functions. As dB levels increase, the body responds with greater cardiovascular responses characteristic of stress (Kryter, 1970). Such reactions as increased heart rate or increased blood pressure become evident.

As chronic dB levels approach 85 dB, significant potential for permanent hearing loss increases. Perhaps the most insidious aspect of this destructive process is that chronic noise exposure is typically selective in its degenerative attack on auditory acuity. The usual case of hearing loss occurs only on specific frequency levels depending upon the frequency of the exposure. Therefore, it may be very difficult for a worker to become aware of a hearing loss until it evolves to a state of major significance.

The federal government has mandated that workers exposed to an average 8-hour level of 90 dB must wear protective ear equipment.

In addition to the harmful effects caused by the intensity of noise, the frequency can also be a factor. Frequencies in excess of 20,000 Hz are most implicated in the harmful effects of noise. However, it has been shown that frequencies in the 15- to 20-Hz range appear especially stressful because of their ultra-low vibration levels. Such levels appear to adversely affect the internal organs of many humans. In some cases frequency tones between these levels may actually reduce the stressful effects of noise.

Reviews by Kryter (1970) and Glass and Singer (1972) suggest that chronic, unprotected exposure to noise in excess of 90 dB and 20,000 Hz can result in many of the following responses:

Physiological
1. Increased heart rate
2. Increased blood pressure
3. Degenerative hearing processes
4. Decreased white blood cell presence
5. Increased adrenal medullary function
6. Increased adrenal cortical function
7. Increased anxiety caused by massive cortical bombardment

Behavioral
1. Decreased learning ability
2. Increased error rate in simple production tasks
3. Increased frustration
4. Decreased tendency and ability to communicate
5. Decreased ability to concentrate
6. Decreased vigilance
7. Decreased ability to gather information
8. Decreased ability to perform analytical functions
9. Decreased short-term memory
10. Increased accident rates

Figure 8.1

Decibel Levels for Exposure to Common Sounds in Business and Industry

Common Sounds	Average dB	Common Sounds	Average dB
Rocket engine	180	Food disposal	85
Air raid siren	140	Inside a noisy restaurant	75
Police and fire siren at 100 feet	135	Inside a stenographic room	75
Jet takeoff at 200 feet	130	Loud conversation at 3 feet	75
Car horn at 3 feet	125	Electric shaver	75
Pneumatic (air) drill at 5 feet	125	Vacuum cleaner	75
Inside a discotheque	125	Noisy office	70
Rock concert	125	Dishwasher	70
Pile drivers at 25 feet	120	Washing machine	70
Inside a boiler room	110	Inside a classroom	68
Train passing at 10 feet	108	Clothes dryer	60
Inside a heavy manufacturing plant	100	Normal conversation at 3 feet	60
Chain saw at 3 feet	100	Average residential street	55
Riveting gun at 25 feet	100	Table fan	50
Garbage truck	100	Refrigerator	40
Gasoline mower	90	Quiet office	40
City traffic at 5 feet	90	Library	38
Outboard motor at 10 feet	85	Soft whisper at 15 feet	25
Home shop tools	85	Hearing begins	0

Figure 8.2

Effects of Noise Levels on Humans

dBLevel	Effect
140+	acute exposures may damage hearing
140	
130	pain threshold
120	
110	
100	
90	
85	hearing loss after repeated 8-hour exposures
80	
70	potential for hearing loss begins
65	evidence of a stress response begins
60	
55	disruption of conversations
50	
40	sleep disrupted
30	
20	
10	
0	hearing begins

How stressed are you by noise intensity? Figure 8.1 contains dB levels for common sources of noise in business and industry. To calculate what your average dB exposure is during a typical 8-hour working day, simply estimate in hours or decimal fractions of hours what portion of your day is spent in exposure to the sources provided. If you cannot find exactly the source of noise to which you are most commonly exposed, base your estimate on similar sources that are provided here. After you calculate a rough 8-hour average daily exposure level, look at Figure 8.2, which summarizes the effects of noise intensity on the human body. What level are you on? Does noise contribute to your level of stress?

Lighting

Lighting within your occupational environment is another potential source of stress. Either too little light or too much light can create a stress response (see Hopkinson and Collins, 1970).

The luminance of a light source may be measured in nits (candles per square meter).

Tasks that involve fine detail in workmanship (such as watchmaking) require a great deal of light. The recommended luminance for such tasks is around 800 to 1,000 nits. General office work and general factory work require around 100 nits. Most stores require around 60 to 100 nits. Finally, hallways usually require around 30 nits.

When lighting is below these recommended minimums, the eyes must strain to accomplish the working tasks. The most common form of stress from eyestrain is muscle tension headaches caused by the muscular adjustments needed to maintain the proper visual acuity.

The most common characteristic of too much light is glare. Glare results from having the light source so bright that it interferes with your focusing upon the object being viewed. In effect, the light source competes within the retina with the object that you are interested in viewing. The result is excessive retinal stimulation, which can be highly frustrating. Glare also appears to cut down on the length of time that a worker can spend at a given task without developing headaches.

Temperature

As most readers will confirm, working conditions that are too hot or too cold can be stressful.

The ideal average temperature (at 50 percent relative humidity) for sedentary work ranges from 70 to 75 degrees Fahrenheit for someone wearing a suit and long-sleeved shirt. Light standing work is done best at about 66 to 72 degrees. Manual labor appears to be done best at a few degrees lower (see McIntyre, 1973).

Ambient temperature in excess of 81 degrees Fahrenheit appears to erode productivity on tasks that consist of complex reasoning or finite detail and concentration. This is especially true in temperatures in excess of 86 degrees Fahrenheit. This productivity decline appears to be due to the psychophysiological arousal characteristic of the stress response. However, it is interesting to note that temperatures in the low 80s have little effect upon light mental tasks such as basic arithmetic or typing, or on light manual tasks such as most production-line work.

In this discussion of heat, it is important to mention humidity. High humidity can significantly increase the stress from heat. The reason is that your body cools itself by evaporation of perspiration. This evaporation process is retarded by high humidity and the result is greater retained heat in your body. Fresh circulating air tends to assist in the cooling process.

Although most of the stress caused by temperature is heat related, cold can also affect industrial performance. As the work environment gets colder, blood flows out of your hands and feet to conserve heat loss by radiation. When this happens you begin to lose fine motor control, and so manual performance is hindered. Such performance declines significantly when hand temperatures drop below 55 degrees Fahrenheit. In general, however, excessive heat appears to be a larger contributor to stress and decreased occupational performance.

Physical Posture

A final consideration within this chapter is the physical position or posture that you find youself in during a working day.

Cramped muscles and inactivity seem to plague white-collar workers. Muscle tension in the head, neck, and shoulders is the most prevalent example of what can happen if you labor over piles of paper every day. Leg cramps and even some lower back problems can result from chronic sitting. Typists know all too well the aching forearms, wrists, and fingers that can result from hours of typing. In addition to these specific problems, the physically stagnant worker must consider the effects of this working condition upon the cardiovascular system. Before too long, exercise programs become a necessity for a healthy mind and body. We will examine exercise in a later chapter.

The physically active blue-collar worker can benefit from a sensibly planned exercise program as well. Even though many blue-collar workers come home fatigued from a tough day of physical labor, seldom do they engage in work which assists in the maintenance of the cardiopulmonary systems. Planned exercise can actually increase strength and energy levels for individuals who work a physically laborious job.

Summary

In summary, the physical environment in which you work can contribute to your stress levels just as the numerous psychosocial stressors we examined can cause you stress. Yet even with unfavorable physical environment, you may be able to help yourself. In Chapter 12 we will discuss specific exercises for cramped muscles, and in Chapter 13 we discuss the role of planned exercise in stress reduction. The variables of noise, lighting, and temperature are harder to control on an individual level than are many of the other factors we've discussed in this book. However, in some cases company-wide effort may help reduce the adverseness of these stress-related factors.

Conclusion

This section has concerned itself with describing common factors which contribute to stress on the job. Table II. 1 is a summary chart entitled Occupational Stress Profile. You may mark on this chart your scores from Exercise 1 through 6 so as to yield a graphic summary of your relationship with these stressors. You should remember that these exercises are designed to promote greater

Table II. 1
OCCUPATIONAL STRESS PROFILE

	Overload	Inactivity and Boredom	Frustration	Change	Type A	Diet
Excessive Stress Level	.12 .11 .10 .9 .8 .7 .6 .5 .4	.10 .9 .8 .7 .6 .5 .4 .3	.15 .14 .13 .12 .11 .10 .9 .8 .7 .6 .5 .4	.16 .15 .14 .13 .12 .11 .10 .9 .8 .7 .6 .5 .4	.14 .13 .12 .11 .10 .9 .8 .7 .6 .5	.6 .5 .4 .3 .2
	.3 .2 .1 .0	.2 .1 .0	.3 .2 .1 .0	.3 .2 .1 .0	.4 .3 .2 .1 .0	.1 .0

awareness; these are **not** to be considered as clinical diagnostic tests.

After completing this part of the book, you should have a better understanding of the factors that may contribute to occupational stress. It should be apparent that most of the stressors are ubiquitous necessities or even rewards of business. Therefore, your focus, based upon the insights provided in Part II, should be on how best to develop a strategy for managing occupational stress, that is, to keep stress from being a debilitating force within your organization, either for yourself or for those who work with you. This task will become simpler with the insight you've gained into the sources of stress from Part II and the recommendations for stress management that will be made in Part III.

PART III
INTERVENTION AND MANAGEMENT TECHNIQUES

Introduction

The remaining chapters of the book are devoted to making you the winner in your fight against excessive stress. You can do this by using your newly acquired knowledge about stress to help you deal with your personal stress in the most healthful and productive ways possible.

The following chapters contain strategies that have proven themselves effective as stress management techniques. They will allow you to interact with on-the-job stress in a more constructive manner and thereby avoid situations in which stress becomes a debilitating and dangerous force.

To achieve this goal of a constructive interface with occupational stress, we have tested numerous stress management techniques over the last several years. Our conclusion is that there is **no single best** stress management technique for all individuals. You are a unique person. Because of your special biological, personality, occupational, and familial characteristics, stress management should be a personalized process. The most effective stress management programs are programs designed **by** you, especially **for** you. We have designed a framework which allows you to develop the stress management system that will be maximally effective for your personal needs. We call this framework "The Holistic System for Controlling Stress and Tension." It is a system which takes into consideration the complexities of the human personality and of the business and industrial environments.

The basis for our Holistic System is the fact that occupational stress may be handled in any combination of four different ways. First, through Human Engineering and Personality Engineering, you can learn to avoid or otherwise change your relationship to your stressors. Second, through the consistent practice of relaxation exercises, you can actually stabilize and reinforce your psychophysiological reactions to your stressors. Third, you can learn to utilize the products of the stress response and instill in yourself feelings of tranquility and accomplishment through regular physical exercise. And finally, through the Organizational Stress Audit, it becomes possible to reduce occupational stress at the source—the organization itself.

The Holistic System

I. Avoid Stressors
   Human Engineering; Personality Engineering
II. Increase Psychophysiological Stability
   Relaxation Techniques
III. Utilize the Products of the Stress Response
   Exercise Programs
IV. Modify Organizational Stressors
   Organizational Stress Audit

We will describe in detail numerous specific techniques under each of the subheadings.

As you read this part of the book, match your preferences and needs to the stress reduction strategies that best suit you, seeing how these strategies may be adopted into your lifestyle. Be thinking of possible alterations you may have to make in order to fit these techniques to you and your living and working conditions.

The key to the quickest and most effective personal results is **daily** use of one or two techniques from **each** of the first three major headings. In this way you will create your own personalized stress reduction program that will combat excessive stress on three levels simultaneously. As an effective complement to these strategies for personal stress management (which are effective in any organizational setting), the Organizational Stress Audit directs corrective action toward the organization itself. This combination of personal and organizational stress management strategies represents a truly holistic system.

Chapter 9

Human Engineering

In today's "age of anxiety" most of us have grown accustomed to passively accepting the stressfulness of day-to-day living. Few of us even consider the possibility that perhaps some of the stressors in our lives could be effectively restructured, or even **avoided**, so as to eliminate much of our stress at its source. Whenever possible, avoiding the stressor is usually the most efficient and effective strategy for managing stress. The most common response to such a proposal, however, is a pessimistic "It's impossible for me to change my job!" While that may be true for most of us, it **is** possible to change the way that you carry out your job! In this chapter we will introduce you to what we call Human Engineering strategies. These are techniques that you may use to restructure the way you undertake your job. In effect, Human Engineering merely refers to psychoenvironmental manipulations of your stressors that will make your job less stressful.

Many of us are guilty of overloading ourselves with work. We may be wishing to impress the boss with our hard work, or we may simply be trying to make a few more dollars. Pretty soon our attitude becomes one of expecting these high levels of stress and strain along with their rewards. We then run the risk of developing a "Superman" attitude, that is, an "I can do **anything**" self-image. While sometimes constructive, this attitude too often motivates us to take on more and more challenges until we eventually erode our mental and physical health to the point where some form of breakdown becomes a certainty.

Our research has suggested that by quantifying and organizing the demands placed upon you, you will be able more healthfully and productively to respond to these demands. One system of doing just that is a combined Work-By-Objectives and Time Management system. These two strategies have been found effective in combating stress from overload as well as stress from inactivity and boredom.

Work-By-Objectives

The Work-By-Objectives (WBO) strategy is one of the techniques which fall in the Management-By-Objectives genre. WBO represents a strategy which focuses human energy in a reasonable and organized direction (see Drucker, 1954).

The mechanics of the WBO strategy are as follows. At the beginning of some calendar or fiscal period you would sit down and formulate the objectives (goals) that you wish to accomplish for that period. In doing so, make sure that these objectives can be quantified and measured. When you select your objectives it is important to consider the feasibility of the objectives. Ask yourself the question, "Are these objectives reasonable?" Your objectives are unreasonable if they represent too great an increase in performance over your previous performance history. A 20 percent performance increase per year is within reason. More important, your objectives are unreasonable if you are unable to set aside one-eighth of your total time commitment (including work, family, and other domestic requirements) for a **mental health break**. A mental health break is some amount of uninterrupted time (a day, two or three 2 to 4-hour breaks per week) that you can devote to some complete relaxation. It may be engaging in some activity that is truly relaxing, or it may be doing absolutely nothing without having to feel guilty.

Once you're convinced that your objectives are measurable **and** reasonable, your next step is to design a set of plans, actions, or methods by which you can achieve these objectives.

Next, devise a strategy by which you can measure your success in achieving your objectives at the end of the specified period.

It is often a good idea to submit your plans at this point to someone else (your supervisor or a colleague, for example) who will be able to objectively assess the merits of your plans.

Finally, at the end of the allotted time period you will measure your success in obtaining your objectives. If possible, transform this assessment into a percentage. If you failed to achieve your objective, write down an explanation and then state how this barrier can be avoided in the future so as to increase your probability of success.

Figure 9.1 represents a basic WBO format. Use it as a guide to formulate your first WBO system. Remember, the WBO strategy can be thought of as a broad Human Engineering strategy to solidify and provide a general direction to your working behaviors. The WBO system can also be used with objectives or goals which are nonwork related as well.

Although WBO can be effective by itself, sometimes it is insufficient to engage in such a planning strategy merely to point yourself in the right direction with some broad "how-to-get-there" ideas. For this reason we have found the usefulness of combining

Figure 9.1
WBO Format

Name _____

For Period Beginning _____
And Ending _____

TARGET OBJECTIVES (describe fully)	METHODS TO ACHIEVE OBJECTIVES	WAYS TO MEASURE SUCCESS	% SUCCESS OBTAINED (with explanations)

the WBO strategy with another, far more specific, strategy: Time Management.

Time Management

Time Management is to the specific short run what WBO is to the broader long run. The goal of Time Management is to allow you to make the most constructive and healthful use of your day-to-day time as possible. Effective Time Management has three stages: 1) time analysis, 2) strategies for organizing, and 3) strategies for follow-up (see Adcock, 1970).

Time analysis involves the assessment, prioritizing, and scheduling of your time in relation to the demands that will be placed upon you. Figure 9.2 details this process.

> ### Figure 9.2
>
> ### A Model for Time Analysis
>
> Time Analysis involves matching the best combination of time demands with your supply of available time. The following steps provide a means of achieving that goal.
>
> | TIME DEMANDS | TIME SUPPLY |
> |---|---|
> | 1. List all of the tasks that need to be completed within the given time interval. For example, on Monday consider what things need to be done during the coming week (or day, etc.). | 5. Match the tasks with the available time blocks in such a way as to make use of available time most constructively. |
> | 2. Estimate how much time will be needed to complete **each** task. | 6. Many times you will find that there is simply not enough time available to complete all of the tasks. Therefore, you must prioritize the tasks in order of their importance so that the most important tasks will be completed. If extra time becomes available, you may go on to other, less important, tasks. |
> | 3. Go back and increase each of the time estimates in step 2 by 15–20%. This will provide some cushion for error or for unexpected problems. | |
> | 4. Look at your calendar for the week. Identify the blocks of time available **each day** for completing the necessary tasks. | |

Many management consultants feel that the more subordinates you have working for you, the less time you should schedule for definite utilization. The rest of your time should be allotted for emergencies, and so on. It has been suggested that if you are in a top-management position, no more than 50 percent of your time should be scheduled.

Time Management is made effective through the second stage: **implementing strategies for organizing work loads.** One way of making more time for yourself is to **delegate** responsibilities. There seems to be a hesitancy on the part of many corporate managers to delegate enough of their own work to subordinates. The result is an overburdened, overstressed manager. We have seen this phenomenon in countless organizations. The motivations for choosing not to delegate can be numerous and complex; they may range from an unconscious need to "protect" one's job, to lack of faith in one's subordinates. In the long run, however, failure to delegate responsibilities takes its toll in the manager's health and the job dissatisfaction of his/her subordinates. Another strategy for effective time organization is **segmentation**. Segmentation involves placing tasks that require similar environments, resources, etc., all together so as to maximize efficiency. Finally, it is often a wise strategy on your part to **minimize interruptions and distractions** while you are working. Distractions foster inefficiency and mistakes.

The last stage of Time Management is formulating a **strategy for follow-up**. Follow-up involves making a regular assessment of the efficiency of your time analysis and organizing stages. Follow-up gives you the opportunity to adjust these strategies for the best possible fit to your personality and job.

The WBO and Time Management system just examined represents a way of organizing and directing your supply of time so that you are able to maximize your potential for achieving your career goals with the least stress possible. There exist other Human Engineering strategies that are of further help in reducing stress, however.

Determining Your Optimal Stress Level

As we saw in an earlier section, stress can be positive or negative depending upon the quantity. Figure 9.3 depicts the relationship between stress arousal and performance. As stress increases, so does performance. This **eustress**, described by Hans Selye, is an energizing or motivating force. However, when the stress arousal becomes too great, it will lead to a debilitating effect and performance will decline. This level of stress is called **distress**.

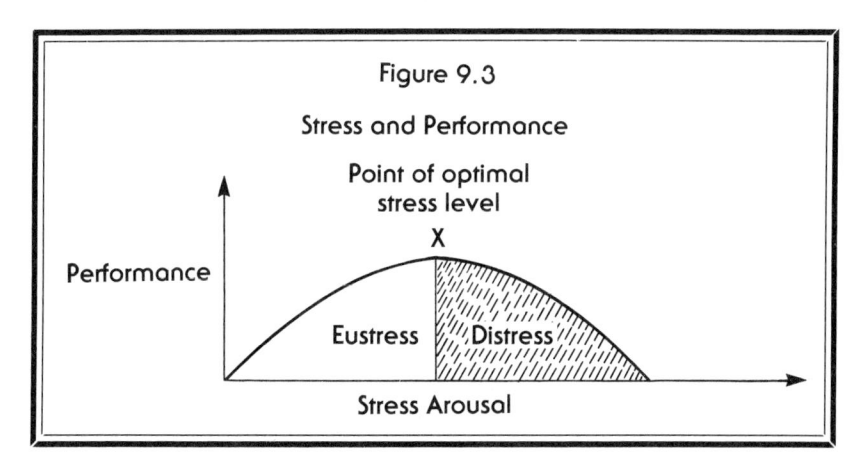

Figure 9.3

Stress and Performance

The X point represents the **point of optimal stress**, that is, the point at which stress is motivating the worker to the point of highest performance. However, when this level is exceeded, and stress continues to increase, the effect is to quickly force a decline in performance.

The strategy of identifying the optimal stress level is an important one for business and industry. It acts as a barometer to tell you when you are "distressing" yourself due to overload (perhaps the most common error people make). Similarly, the prudent manager can become skilled at identifying these signs of distress in his/her employees and thereby avert overload and performance declines.

Unfortunately, there are no absolute formulas for identifying the optimal stress point. This point is idiosyncratic, that is, it varies from person to person and from situation to situation. However, we can give you some rough clues on how to go about finding your optimal stress level.

The best way to find your optimal stress level is to **recognize the signs of distress** and to continue to reduce your stress to the point where these signs disappear. That, by definition, will be your optimal stress level. While this strategy seems simple, it is not easy to accomplish because most people have become immune, or have lost their innate sensitivity for excessive stress. This section will help you to become, once again, sensitive to the signs of distress.

Even though the signs of stress are unique to each of us to some degree, there are some general clues that will usually indicate the existence of excessive stress. There are three main types of stress manifestations, that is, areas where stress will show itself. The specific cues, called the **signs of distress**, encompass 1) mood, 2) visceral, and 3) musculoskeletal signs.

Stress often becomes recognizable by the **mood** or **disposition** of a person. Feelings of worry, nervousness, overexcitability, and insecurity are all common mood reactions of distress. Many individuals, when asked to describe their thoughts during distress, report racing thoughts, being rattled or ill-at-ease, or being generally "uncomfortable." Insomnia is a common reaction as well.

Another major area within which stress will strike is the **viscera**, controlled by the autonomic nervous system. Signs of visceral reactions during stress are such symptoms as cold chills, feeling faint or light-headed, a dry mouth, upset or "sinking" stomach, or a ringing in the ears. Some individuals report heart flutterings, or a flushing of the face and neck.

Finally, distress becomes most outwardly apparent when it strikes the **musculoskeletal** system. Common signs of this kind of stress reaction are trembling fingers and hands, muscle twitching, muscular tension or tightness, stammering or stuttering of speech, and any other difficulties in fine motor control.

Figure 9.4 summarizes these clues to distress. Check the signs that seem to be most frequent for you during periods of distress.

Figure 9.4
What Are Your "Signs of Distress"?

MOOD AND DISPOSITION SIGNS
- _____ I become overexcited
- _____ I worry
- _____ I feel insecure
- _____ I have difficulty sleeping at night
- _____ I become easily confused and forgetful
- _____ I become very uncomfortable and ill-at-east
- _____ I become nervous

MUSCULOSKELETAL SIGNS
- _____ My fingers and hands shake
- _____ I can't sit or stand still
- _____ I develop twitches
- _____ My head begins to ache
- _____ I feel my muscles become tense or stiff
- _____ I stutter or stammer when I speak
- _____ My neck becomes stiff

VISCERAL SIGNS
- _____ My stomach becomes upset
- _____ I feel my heart pounding
- _____ I sweat profusely
- _____ My hands become moist
- _____ I feel light-headed or faint
- _____ I experience cold chills
- _____ My face becomes "hot"
- _____ My mouth becomes dry
- _____ I experience ringing in my ears
- _____ I get a sinking feeling in my stomach

By completing the chart in Figure 9.4, you can obtain an idea as to how you respond to stress. If you make note of these signs, you can recognize distress early, in yourself and others, thus increasing the possibility of reducing the overload before it causes harm. This identification procedure will also quickly point out the optimal stress point. As soon as these signs materialize, the optimal stress point has been passed and further stress will be harmful. It is at this point that easing off your work will actually be the most productive thing you can do. If you are a manager and see these things occurring in your employees, you would be wise to lessen their work load. You will save the employee, yourself, and the company time and money.

Nutritional Engineering

Our fast-moving society has dictated a secondary role to nutrition. In evidence to this fact you need merely count the number of "fast food" establishments as you drive. In addition we have witnessed the decline, to virtual extinction, of the family-centered meal. Unfortunately, many nutritionists feel that the actual quality of our meals has declined along with their sociological importance.

We outlined earlier the evidence pointing to the fact that your diet can actually increase your stress levels. With this fact in mind, we feel that you can actually reduce some of your stress through a conscious effort to manipulate your diet. We call these dietary manipulations Nutritional Engineering.

The first strategy in the area of nutrition is to avoid foods that initiate a stress response. Earlier we discussed the stimulant chemicals caffeine and nicotine. These chemicals actually create a stress response within your body if consumed in sufficient quantity. In smaller quantities they can certainly exacerbate a stress reaction if one is already initiated. Foods that are high in sympathomimetics are coffee, tea, chocolate, cocoa, many cola beverages, and, although not a food, tobacco products. These items should be avoided, or at least minimized, during stressful periods and when relaxation is desired.

Our society has developed a "chronic sweet tooth"; sugar represents a major portion of our calorie intake every day. Highly refined sugars have been implicated in contributing to nervousness and anxiety through the depletion of B vitamins from our bodies. While the total avoidance of foods containing refined sugar is not recommended, foods with natural sugars may be substituted at times. For example, fresh fruits make excellent desserts in lieu of pies or cakes. Honey can be used as a sweetener in lieu of refined sugar. Such manipulations will depend on your eating habits and tastes.

Related to this issue of vitamin depletion is the fact that many people have begun taking vitamin supplements to combat the ill effects of stress. If your diet is lacking necessary vitamins or if you are suffering from some form of vitamin deficiency, you might consider vitamin supplements.

There exist many excellent multivitamins on the over-the-counter market, and many are reasonably priced. Synthetic vitamins appear to be just as useful to the body as the more expensive "natural" vitamin sources. There is no need to invest in exotic vitamin regimens. It has been suggested that the American urine is the most expensive in the world because of its high concentration of excessive vitamins. And it is important to realize that excessive consumption of some vitamins can be toxic, specifically the fat-soluble vitamins—A, D, E, and K—because levels can be stored in the body. However, if you feel that your diet lacks sufficient vitamins or that you are under extreme stress, vitamin supplements may be a consideration. Some companies have even marketed a specific "stress vitamin" capsule which is high in the vitamins depleted by the stress reaction. It is always a good idea, however, to consult a knowledgeable physician before taking any dietary supplement or drastically altering your diet.

Table 9.1 lists the Recommended Daily Allowance (RDA) average adult ranges for selected vitamins which are depleted from the body during excessive stress reactions.

Table 9.1
Adult RDA for Stress-Related Vitamins

Folic acid	400 mcg
Thiamine	1.0–1.5 mg
Riboflavin	1.3–1.7 mg
Niacin	13.0–18.0 mg
Pantothenic acid	.5–10.0 mg
Pyridoxine HCl	1.5–1.8 mg
Choline	unknown
Vitamin C	45.0–60.0 mg

Table 9.2 lists the usual supplemental ranges for the same selected vitamins.

Table 9.2
Daily Supplementary Ranges for Stress-Related Vitamins

Folic acid	1,000–10,000 mcg
Thiamine	2–10 mg
Riboflavin	2–10 mg
Niacin	50–5,000 mg
Pantothenic acid	20–100 mg
Pyridoxine HCl	4–550 mg
Choline	100–1,000 mg
Vitamin C	250–5,000 mg*

*Intake above 5,000 mg a day may produce some undesirable effects.

A final Nutritional Engineering strategy to minimize dietary contributions to stress is to modify your salt (sodium chloride) intake. Excessive sodium consumption contributes to fluid retention and elevated blood pressure.

Since everyone's dietary needs are different, you should not drastically restrict sodium chloride consumption without consulting your physician. However, as a guide to general food consumption, Table 9.3 lists foods that are high in sodium. Table 9.4 lists seasonings that may be used in low-sodium diets. Consider, as well, the use of potassium chloride (salt substitute) for flavoring your meals instead of regular table salt.

Table 9.3
Foods High in Sodium

Most Canned:	Pork Products:	Snack Foods:
meats	ham	pretzels
soups	bacon	popcorn
stews	sausage	potato chips
sauerkraut	hot dogs	

Cheeses:
  processed cheese
  cheese dips
  snacking cheese spreads

Most quick-order foods at drive-in restaurants

Seasonings:
  prepared mustard
  catsup
  Worcestershire sauce
  soy sauce
  pickles
  relishes
  meat tenderizers
  peanut butter (most brands are heavy in sodium additives)

Baking soda (sodium bicarbonate contains about 1,000 mg sodium per level teaspoon).

As a rule, processed foods contain more sodium than do fresh foods.

Table 9.4
Seasonings That May Be Used in Low-Sodium Diets

Almond extract	Ginger	Paprika
Bay leaf	Lemon	Parsley
Caraway seed	Lime	Pepper
Chili powder	Maple extract	Pimento
Chives	Mint	Sage
Cinnamon	Mustard (dry)	Sesame seeds
Cloves	Nutmeg	Thyme
Coconut	Orange extract	Vanilla extract
Curry	Oregano	Vinegar

When Nutritional Engineering is used as one of the Social Engineering strategies, it can prove to be a powerful addition to the holistic paradigm for stress control. You may follow the suggestions provided earlier, or you may expand and create your own.

Summary

The Human Engineering strategies summarized in Table 9.5 represent ways for you to reduce the stress in your life by altering the sources of your stress. Find the ones that are best for you and use them on a regular basis. The results will be higher performance and better health.

Table 9.5
Human Engineering Strategies

I. Working-By-Objectives (WBO)
II. Establishing a Mental Health Break
III. Time Management
   A. Time Analysis
   B. Organization
      1. Delegation
      2. Segmentation
      3. Eliminating Distractions
   C. Follow-up Reassessment
IV. Determining Your Optimal Stress Levels
V. Nutritional Engineering
   A. Reducing sympathomimetics
   B. Reducing refined sugar consumption
   C. Vitamin supplementation
   D. Reducing sodium intake

Chapter 10

Personality Engineering

Many of you by now have decided that your personality is contributing to much of the stress in your life. If so, there are strategies that you can utilize that will allow you effectively to alter your personality and make your life less stressful. In this chapter we will offer some suggestions on how you may achieve this goal through various techniques called Personality Engineering.

As we stated earlier, your personality consists of your values, attitudes, and behavior patterns. **Values** are those rigid, deep-grained evaluations of good and bad. Because they come from your parents and other "significant others" in your life, they are often somewhat resistant to change. **Attitudes** are usually less rigid perceptions, or points of view, concerning your environment. Finally, **behavior patterns** are your overt expressions and the way you conduct yourself. By changing your personality, you are to some degree restructuring the things that are characteristically **you**—your values, attitudes, and behavior patterns. We have selected the term Personality Engineering to refer to any attempt to alter some aspect of your personality with the goal of making your job and your life less stressful.

Hans Selye has suggested that perhaps the most powerful stress reduction technique of all is adopting a positive attitude toward your stressors. Sometimes this may mean finding the good in adversity (every cloud has a silver lining). Sometimes this may mean making conscious efforts to change your personality structure.

Let us consider those personality traits found to be the most costly in the business world—the constellation of traits known as the Type A Personality. We noted earlier that the Type A Personality consists of a set of stressful personality traits which have been found to be not only harmful, but highly prevalent in the working world. They are inappropriate time urgency, inappropriate polyphasic behavior, hostility, and a too frequent tendency to undertake a task without really knowing how to get the job done. Singularly, any one of these traits can be harmful to your job performance and your health; collectively, they represent the fully developed Type A Personality that in most cases has been demonstrated to be a very destructive force not only for your health but for your company as well. We have compiled a series of strategies designed to help you constructively modify any or all of these four stressful personality traits.

A significant number of people in our society suffer from the two most common stress-related personality traits: the "hurry sickness" (inappropriate time urgency) and the need to do more than one thing at a time (polyphasic behavior). To overcome the inappropriate expression of these tendencies, the skills in Time Management and Work-By-Objectives are both quite effective.

Time Management

As we have already discussed, Time Management is the process of utilizing your time in the most effective and least stressful way. It involves assessing your time requirements, prioritizing tasks which need to be done, and properly scheduling those tasks as well as the other components mentioned earlier in the text (see Human Engineering).

WBO

Work-By-Objectives (WBO) may be considered a macrocosmic view of Time Management. It involves developing realistic short- and/or long-term task objectives in addition to procedures for measuring success.

Because both Time Management and WBO were discussed in detail in the previous chapter on Human Engineering, you can refer back to that section for the specifics of how these strategies may be implemented. Of equal importance, however, is for you to understand the reason that Time Management and WBO are effective in combating time urgency and polyphasic behavior: these strategies place all of the probable demands on your time and energy right before your eyes, "up-front" where there are few chances for overburdening yourself. You have even built in a time cushion for unanticipated emergencies. Therefore with this information concerning your time,
1. You have a realistic and obtainable schedule for the utilization of your time and work energies.
2. You no longer have to endlessly rush around saving time "just in case."
3. Most important, you are less prone to perceive yourself as a "Superman," capable of taking on any and all work assignments, because you now know how the demands on you translate into actual time and energy expenditures. In effect, you now possess a realistic evaluation of your current limitations.

Hostility and overly competitive/aggressive behavior represent another stressful personality trait. We have found two techniques effective in teaching chronically hostile individuals to reduce this hostility/aggression syndrome: 1) gaining awareness of the nature and cause of hostility, and 2) "switching places."

Understanding Hostility

The effectiveness of the technique of gaining awareness of hostility is based upon the fact that, when most people are made aware of the dangerous effects of hostility as an emotion and are given insight into the cause of their hostility, their hostility quickly disappears.

Hostility is an emotion which affects you adversely. Physiologically, hostility is characterized primarily by significant increases in the secretion of the hormone norepinephrine, which causes a tightening of your peripheral blood vessels. The end result is to elevate your blood pressure. This action forces your heart to work harder than it should. Frequent hostility has been implicated as one of the causes of essential hypertension. Psychologically, hostility fosters confusion and resentment.

As for the cause of hostility, Milton Layden (1977) provides us with significant insight in his book **Escaping the Hostility Trap**. Layden tells us that hostility is caused by feelings of inferiority. In other words, you become hostile because someone or something has placed you in a position where your self-esteem has been devalued, or where you see others losing their respect for you. Because your ego is your most vulnerable commodity, your hostility usually results in a need to demonstrate superiority as kind of a way to compensate for ("redeem") your lost respect. Unfortunately, your attempts to demonstrate superiority will usually result in embarrassing someone else (which causes hostility to be directed toward you), or others may simply perceive that you are a "show-off." Neither situation really proves constructive; in fact you probably end up looking worse, and this position will simply rekindle the hostility cycle. This sequence is illustrated in Figure 10.1.

Now that you have this information concerning the nature and cause of hostility, the next time you notice yourself becoming hostile and angry here in four steps is a way for you to put this knowledge to work:

1. **Remember** that those feelings are based upon feelings of inferiority.
2. **Search** for the specific cause of your inferiority feelings. (If

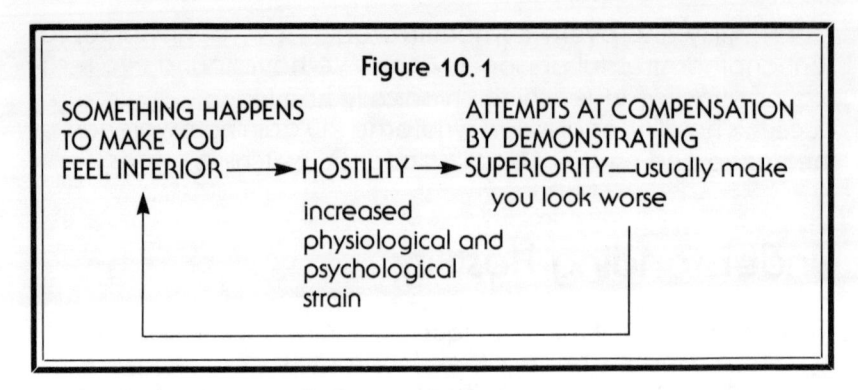

```
┌─────────────────────────────────────────────────────────────┐
│                       Figure 10.1                           │
│   SOMETHING HAPPENS              ATTEMPTS AT COMPENSATION   │
│   TO MAKE YOU                    BY DEMONSTRATING           │
│   FEEL INFERIOR ──▶ HOSTILITY ──▶ SUPERIORITY—usually make  │
│         ▲             increased      you look worse         │
│         │             physiological and                     │
│         │             psychological                         │
│         │             strain                                │
│         └──────────────────────────────┘                    │
└─────────────────────────────────────────────────────────────┘
```

someone else's hostility provoked you, just remember that they are reacting to their own feelings of inferiority.)
3. **Understand** how self-destructive hostility as an emotion really is, and how it can lead to a cycle of hostility.
4. Pride yourself on the fact that you are a superior enough person to recognize the foolishness in hostility.

Switching Roles

Our second technique for reducing excessive aggression is based upon developing empathy skills, that is, learning to feel as someone else feels. We call the technique **switching places**.

If you are this overly aggressive individual, you probably have a tendency to usurp the rights of others around you, most times unconsciously so, by merely failing to consider the impact or consequences of your own actions. To combat this tendency to act first and think about the consequences later, we have trained people to put themselves "in the other person's shoes." By developing your empathy skills you can become more sensitive to the needs and feelings of others (a necessity for effective managers).

The exercise below is one we've found helpful in assisting individuals to consider the needs of others.

Switching Roles

The next time you have a decision to make or some action to carry out that significantly affects those around you, do the following:
1. From your vantage point as yourself, write down at least **two** positive effects that your behavior will have on those around you.
2. Next, from that same vantage point write down at least **two** negative effects that your behavior will have on those around you.

3. Switch roles: if someone did to you what you are doing to those around you, how would you feel? Write down **two** positive effects and then write down **two** negative effects.

After a while, this exercise has the effect of teaching you to **automatically** consider the rights and feelings of those around you without having to force yourself to write these things down.

Goal Path Model

In order to combat the tendency for individuals to rush into projects without proper preparation, we have found training in organization and planning to be effective. In Figure 10.2 you will find a simple schema designed to promote thoughts toward adequate planning. Although it is a basic model, you will find it helpful in starting you on your way to successful planning and organizing skills. Try it out!

Figure 10.2

THE GOAL PATH MODEL

STEP 1. Define the task.
Can the task be broken down into smaller subtasks?

NO	YES
Continue to analyze the task.	List each subtask and complete the rest of this form for each subtask.

STEP 2. What personnel or help will be needed? LIST.
STEP 3. What are possible sources for personnel?
STEP 4. What materials will be needed? LIST.
STEP 5. What are possible sources for materials?
STEP 6. Estimate costs for steps 2 and 4.
STEP 7. Estimate time required.
STEP 8. Hypothesize possible obstacles.
STEP 9. For each obstacle, go back and develop at least one contingency plan, more if possible.
STEP 10. BEGIN!

Relaxation

Finally, and most important in successfully modifying the entire Type A personality, is the practice of some form of relaxation technique on a **regular** and **consistent** basis. The most commonly used techniques are meditation, neuromuscular relaxation, and biofeedback methodologies. The subsequent chapters in this book will discuss relaxation methods that we have found useful for the stressed business person.

Conclusion

Undertaking the challenge of changing your personality is one of the most formidable tasks in the field of human behavior. These Type A personality traits seem to be a particularly difficult structure to alter. The major reason for this resistance to change is the fact that the Type A individual usually views his/her success in the business world as a direct result of the Type A traits; therefore, giving up these traits is falsely interpreted as giving up success. Because Type A behaviors grew out of, and are closely related to, traditional business behaviors that are attributes leading to success, individuals think success is a function of Type A personality. The crucial difference between the Type A personality traits and these attributes is that Type A traits represent radical **extremes** of the traditional business attributes. A brief review of the Type A behaviors will attest to this conclusion. Notice that most of the Type A traits could prove productive, if used in milder degrees. Therefore, if the Type A individual is successful in business it will be **in spite of** the Type A personality, **not because of** it.

The motivations to undertake an alteration in the Type A personality are substantial. By modifying these Type A personality traits, you will not only reduce your stress levels but also increase your on-the-job performance, for the following reasons:

1. Confusion and anxiety from self-imposed time urgency will decrease for you and those who must interact with you.
2. Interpersonal cooperation will increase because of a decline in your overzealousness and hostility.
3. Mistakes caused by a) rushing into projects without proper direction, or b) attempting to complete too many tasks at once, will decline.
4. Fatigue will decrease.
5. Sick time usually decreases.
6. Productive longevity will usually increase.

Summary

The key to successfully modifying these Type A personality traits is in choosing a combination of the preceding strategies (Table 10.1)—in effect, choosing a personalized program that you feel is best suited for you. The only way that these strategies will succeed, however, is if you practice them **consistently**. Only through regular, consistent practice will these strategies be effective in modifying the Type A traits that you have developed over the years. So don't expect immediate success. Rather, develop your program and wait **patiently**. After a month or so you will begin to notice subtle positive changes taking place in your personality. After four months the changes will still **seem** subtle, but the effect on your job and your health will be very rewarding.

Table 10.1
Personality Engineering Strategies
To Reduce Type A Behavior

I. Time Management
II. WBO
III. Understanding Hostility
IV. Switching Roles
V. Goal Path Model
VI. Relaxation

Chapter 11

Roads to Relaxation

(The Foundations of the Matrix Relaxation Program)

More than being a road **to** relaxation, the trail we are traversing here is a road **back**, since relaxation and tranquility represent our normal, natural state of being. With the increasing complexity of society there came more complex strategies of coping and maintaining balance. There has developed a vicious cycle, until now the coping behavior engenders as much stress as the stressor. We wear many masks, we play many roles, we plan, we worry, we dream. Because relaxation is a natural state of being, the techniques to reduce stress and tension should be mentally and physically simple, restoring balance to the organism.

Because of the nature of our lifestyle, most of us must work to maintain our tranquility. Those who do not understand the true nature of the balance or relaxed state continue to use complex and unnatural methods to obtain it. This unit will present a brief overview of some of the popular techniques which are not *in toto* contained in the alleviation chapter of this book, although it should be realized that the underlying principles of many techniques are universal ideas which transcend numerous methodologies. We have simplified the complex, using time-observed philosophies and teaching techniques to build the Matrix Relaxation Program.

Drugs, Including Alcohol

The drug-induced altered state of consciousness is more often than not a pleasant experience, but the relationship to relaxation is tenuous. The intensity or quality of the experience depends upon such factors as when and even where the drug is consumed, the quantity and quality of the product, the mood of the user, the motivation for using the drug, and the user's general state of health, especially his/her emotional well-being. Drugs do change one's state of consciousness, but do they promote relaxation? The answer is sometimes yes and sometimes no. Drugs can change awareness, memory, emotions, and moods. These changes can obscure obligations and goals and reduce the anxiety of time pressures. The sense of unrealness and lack of ego involvement are calming, but the learned tendency of the mind to create logic and order often intervenes, creating alterations in moods that oscillate between pleasure and apprehension.

If drugs do promote relaxation, the mechanisms of action must be to block the awareness of the event, and/or to change the significance or importance you attach to it. The drug creates a temporary block in that you are not actively thinking about the problem. Unfortunately, the problem still exists; it is stored in various parts of the brain and is producing feeling and other body alterations which go on even though you are not actively thinking about it. In the final analysis, stress is a physiological state of response to psychosocial events. The psychoactive drugs, both legal and illegal, that one might typically consume to promote relaxation do not change body physiology. The problem is still present, and it continues to stress the system; the only difference is that we have temporarily blocked the situation from active, here-and-now thoughts.

As you will soon learn, the techniques of stress control are relatively simple activities, but they are active rather than passive. Drugs are passive and uncontrollable; further, whereas a moderate amount taken in social situations may be refreshing and "relaxing," in reality it is the situation and not the drug which is the active ingredient. One needs control of one's thoughts, feelings, and reasoning processes in order to deal with problems.

Mind-Directed States

There are a myriad of currently popular techniques which aim to promote relaxation through mind direction or control. Meditation, yoga, autogenic training, muscular relaxation, and biofeedback are but a few. The **Matrix Relaxation Program** presented in the next chapter is derived from the basic principles of these techniques and it would be advantageous to possess a basic understanding of them. Thus, a brief description of these techniques and their relationship to stress control and relaxation is appropriate here.

Meditation

Meditation—by far the most popular of the mind-directed states—is a state of mind and not really a technique. There are many techniques for reaching that state of mind. In fact, that same mental state can be induced by the other techniques discussed here—yoga, muscular relaxation, biofeedback, and autogenic training. While it is sometimes difficult to separate meditation the **technique** from meditation the **state**, this discussion is warranted since there are numerous such techniques currently flooding the marketplace. It is important to realize that the differences in meditation techniques represent minor differences in style rather than substance or philosophy.

Modern meditative practices represent a mixture of philosophies and techniques descended from ancient yoga and Zen Buddhism. Regardless of their ancestry, all the meditative techniques have two general common phases: a quiet body and a quiet mind. One cannot relax or quiet the mind if the brain is being bombarded with stimulation of tense muscle and hyperactive glands. Thus, elaborate exercises, postures, and other rituals were developed in an attempt to slow the body activities to a point where the mind would also be allowed to become quiet. The primary goal is to reduce what is referred to as the surface chatter of the mind, that is, the constant thinking in the form of planning, remembering, and fantasizing which seems to occupy our every waking moment and keeps us implanted in our ego consciousness. If one can reduce this surface chatter—or in other words, reduce the thoughts of self—anxiety will be reduced, general arousal will be reduced, and the mind can periodically achieve peace and quiet.

Research has shown that during meditation the activity of most physical systems is reduced. Thus, unlike drugs, meditation does seem to induce physical relaxation. At the same time, the meditator is in complete control of the experience and has control over emotions, feelings, and memories. Although meditation is a passive state of mind, it is an active process that takes thought, preparation, and practice.

Common to all meditation are concentration and the closely related techniques of contemplation and mental repetition. Concentration demands control over the mind's tendency to daydream and flip from one ego-related thought to another. The technique of meditation includes a myriad of ways to help learn concentration. The most widely used is the verbal or mental repetition of a word or sound called a **mantra**. A mantra can be a single word such as "om" (a Sanskrit word meaning to be "whole" or "one"), considered to be the universal mantra, or a phrase from the teachings of ancient yoga masters. Herbert Benson, who westernized meditation in his book **The Relaxation Response**, uses simply the word "one." Benson de-ritualized meditation, thus giving a technique to those who felt uncomfortable with the Eastern philosophy and rituals. Other teachers feel the rituals add a sense of motivation to the practice. It is really a matter of style and philosophy.

Meditation is a simple, natural process which can produce results **if it is used.** Each approach purports to be superior in the way that it motivates potential users. For some reason it is difficult for Westerners to maintain the discipline of continued practice. The Western mind is used to being occupied and stimulated. We were not taught to sit quietly without reading or watching television. Even though it is easy to learn, meditation has not really been effective for Westerners as it takes a different mental set than what we have been conditioned to use. This is not to say it cannot be effective; it is only pointing out some inherent difficulties which make the commitment to practice more necessary. One viable alternative can be found in the Relaxation Matrix, which includes exercises using the basics of meditation woven into a program more attuned to Western learning and lifestyles.

Yoga

The word **yoga** is derived from the Sanskrit root meaning "union" or "reunion" and is a method of physical, mental, and spiritual development based on the philosophies of Lord Krishna. Knowledge was passed from enlightened master to student, generation after generation for thousands of years before the first written record appeared around 200 B.C. in Patanjali's Sutras. Since then thousands of books have been written describing the many types of yoga, called "paths," which have developed into spiritual schools and which in many instances have become distinctly separate schools in themselves. Raja Yoga, or Royal Yoga, the path to self-realization and enlightenment, is very similar to the meditative practice described earlier. The most popular path in the Western world is Hatha Yoga, which uses positions and exercises to promote physical and mental harmony. Most yoga practice starts with Hatha Yoga, as it is said to provide the body with health and endurance needed to learn more advanced forms of yoga. Hatha Yoga is practiced for its own rewards, which include strength, flexibility, and reduction of muscle tension, and is used as a technique to quiet the body in preparation for quiet mental states.

Again, one must realize that yoga masters come from a different culture in which both physical structure and physical activity patterns are significantly different from those of Western cultures. Thus, it is difficult for Westerners to completely master all of the positions. Nevertheless, positive results can be derived from yoga, especially if the exercises are chosen for specific outcomes in specific groups of people. For the Relaxation Matrix we have developed some exercises and postures which were derived from the principles of Hatha Yoga. These carefully developed exercises have been shown to yield maximal results in the shortest period of time in groups of individuals with no prior experience or special physical conditioning.

Autogenic Relaxation Training

The term **auto-genesis** (self-generating) describes almost every form of relaxation exercise; however, the name **autogenic** has become synonymous with a form of relaxation involving self-directed mental images of relaxed states. This simple yet advanced technique centers around conditioned patterns of responses which become associated with particular thoughts. Recall those moments when you allow your mind to run away and conjure up a tragic event. You may have heard rumors of turnover in your division, you are summoned to the central office, your thoughts go to demotion or layoff. You build the story in your mind until you can even see yourself telling your coworkers about it. You get chills and the hair raises on the back of your neck. This represents a conditioned physiological response to that particular association. The opposite is also true and also produces a dramatic physiological response. If you imagine yourself in your favorite relaxation spot, perhaps sitting on a quiet beach with the sun warming your body or fishing in your favorite stream, physiologically a relaxation response is triggered. The technique of autogenic relaxation simply helps condition relaxation through self-generated recall of relaxed body states and memories of relaxed times in your life. It is a technique wherein you talk to your body and tell it to relax. It helps if you are able to vividly imagine a scene or feeling in which you have already achieved a quiet physical state. Therefore on the Matrix Relaxation Program the autogenic exercises are preceded by activities that promote physical relaxation.

One of the common techniques used in autogenic relaxation programs capitalizes on the body's ability to follow the commands of the conscious centers of the brain. If you can imagine warmth, or on a feeling level can reproduce a heavy sensation in the limbs, the body has the tendency to reproduce that state. Blood flow in response to the conscious demand will increase to the desired areas thereby creating the desired warmth. This is physiologically impossible without a change in nervous system tone. Thus relaxation is facilitated.

Neuromuscular Relaxation Training

Neuromuscular relaxation training is a program of systematic exercises which train not only the muscles but also the nervous system components which control muscle activity. The objective is to reduce the tension in the muscles; since the muscles make up such a large portion of the body's mass, this reduction represents a significant reduction in total body tension as well. There are literally hundreds of techniques and almost every relaxation program, including the Matrix Relaxation Program presented in this book, utilizes some form of neuromuscular relaxation. The basic objective is to teach the individual to relax the muscles at will by first developing a thinking–feeling awareness of what it is like to be relaxed. If you are able to distinguish between tension and relaxation, control over tension will easily follow. To accomplish this you must learn to center on the task or problem and control the mind's tendency to wander aimlessly in daydreams.

Neuromuscular relaxation requires concentration, but that concentration must be passive in that it must not add to the tension level. Thoughts should be centered on techniques and awareness of tension levels and must not become ego or goal centered. As you perfect your ability, these exercises can be practiced anywhere, even in short periods of usually "wasted" time such as when stopped for a red light or while waiting for an appointment. One drawback to neuromuscular exercise programs in general is that they are time consuming when the aim is to train every muscle in the body individually. We have developed a program that is theoretically based on the concepts of the many techniques which have preceded it; significant differences exist, however, as we use the body's natural knowledge of complete movements of limbs rather than the unnaturalness of individual muscle action used in physical rehabilitation programs.

Biofeedback

Most biofeedback instruments look like sophisticated stereo systems with the addition of a few more wires and cables. Seeing this and reading the science fiction-like accounts of results obtained using biofeedback make it appear somewhat mysterious and magical. However, there is no magic involved in biofeedback as it follows accepted scientific principles; the only real mystery which surrounds its use is the yet unexplained phenomena regarding our seemingly unlimited abilities to regulate and influence our own psychophysiology.

The body's response to stress is a physical release of energy in various forms, most of which are too subtle to be noticed until pain or dysfunction screams for attention. There are definite changes in the cardiovascular system, most noticeably a speeding of the heart rate. Perhaps you have felt the palpitation in your chest. It is common for the hands to become moist with sweat even on the coolest of days. The skin may flush or become excessively pale. Your mouth usually becomes extremely dry but in some instances salivation may increase dramatically. You may become nauseated as your stomach churns with anger. Muscles become excessively tense, making it difficult to breathe or swallow, while your legs threaten to give way. If you have ever felt any of these symptoms, you have experienced biofeedback—the body feeding information about its functioning back to the consciousness centers of your brain.

The simple principle of biofeedback is that awareness of body function is the first and most important ingredient in changing the behavior that caused the stress reaction. Biofeedback is best understood as an educational tool which provides information about behavior or performance in much the same manner as a congratulatory letter from superiors gives feedback on job performance or the bathroom scale gives information about the success of weight reduction efforts. If we learn to listen, our bodies will tell us a lot about its functioning. Biofeedback magnifies the subtle signals so they become more noticeable and can be used simply as a device which trains or attunes our awareness of body language. Thermal measurements of skin temperature can indicate blood flow changes to a particular region of the body. After only a few training sessions one can usually learn to feel the changes without the instrument. Measuring contraction of skeletal muscle can detect muscle action before it reaches the state of producing pain and discomfort. Through training one can usually learn to sense even the most minute change in muscle tension. Likewise, monitoring brain waves can tell us much about states of consciousness and information processing which can aid in the voluntary control of consciousness. The possibilities are as numerous as the systems that can be measured.

In another sense biofeedback is much more than just a self-monitoring system. It can be used to promote self-exploration, self-awareness, and self-control. The training process is in reality a conditioning, or perhaps better stated, a reconditioning process. Relaxation and tranquility condition the tonus of the nervous system to be less reactive, and gradually you begin to change behavior by "becoming" a more tranquil person. The reconditioning or relearning process disciplines the mind to reduce the constant chatter of imagination and anticipation, allowing greater problem-centered concentration and often revealing insights and creativity. What started out as an exercise in relaxation quickly turns into a development of self-awareness and self-control.

To better sense the function of a biofeedback system, try a little experiment. Find your pulse and record a resting pulse rate. Take it for several minutes to be sure you have an accurate reading. Jot down the rate in beats per minute.

_____ beats per minute, resting

Now as you sit quietly, try to imagine a scene or story you find particularly exciting. Really get into it until you can vividly see yourself involved in the situation. After a couple of minutes, stop, take your pulse, and record the beats per minute.

_____ beats per minute, excited

Chances are that if you really got yourself involved in the imagined situation, and if the situation were one you found stressful, you found the second heart rate to be higher than the first. Now relax, quiet your mind, think of a particularly pleasant and tranquil scene. After a couple of minutes take your heart rate again. Chances are it has returned to normal or perhaps is even lower than the first reading.

_____ beats per minute, relaxed

If you could maintain your concentration and vigilance, you could further reduce your heart rate, but you would soon tire of the activity. This is where a biofeedback device helps. It tirelessly monitors and feeds back the heart rate, freeing your mental processes to work on mental exercises and techniques to accelerate the desired results.

Now try another one. Sit back in a chair and try to focus your thoughts on your muscles. Bend your arm up so that your hand touches your shoulder. The muscle tension is obvious as movement occurs. Next, just think of that same movement. You almost have to hold the arm back as it seems to want to move. Feel the muscles contract ever so slightly. Try the same activity with your forehead. Frown, feeling the muscles contract. Then just think of frowning, and feel the tension develop. Next, think of an activity that is unpleasant to you and try to feel the tension which may develop in that area. You are, of course, getting feedback of subtle muscle activity which does not produce movement only because you have not willed the movement. But just as the gross movement can be controlled, so can the more subtle muscle tension if its existence is known. That knowledge is supplied by the electromyograph biofeedback instrument which first senses, then feeds back, information about the tension in a muscle. Through the sensing electrodes placed on the skin over the muscle, the subtle contractions can be measured. The signal is specially processed and converted to a light or sound and is fed back to the individual, who can use that information to direct that muscle to relax. In most tension reduction or general relaxation programs muscles of the face and/or neck are usually used. Tension in these areas generally reflects moods and emotions.

One word of caution: the results reported from many clinical studies are quite sensational. To those who do not understand the interaction of the mind and body or the mechanisms of nervous system control, biofeedback does seem magical. To those hunting for a passive shortcut to nirvana, biofeedback has become the latest fad. But these novitiates have become prey for the small unethical element of our society which seems to be ever-present, offering something for nothing. Even with the advances in electronic technology it is still difficult to obtain anything but very simple temperature trainers for under $400. Cheap equipment may be dangerous if it operates on house current; even when safely battery operated, it is usually ineffective in that the lack of sensitivity and filtering capacity allows for false signals and inaccurate feedback which confuse and retard learning. As always, the best consumer advice is to do your homework and consult with knowledgeable people in the field. Better than buying a home device is organizing a training workshop run by professionals.

Chapter 12

The Matrix Relaxation Program

Stress and tension responses, anxiety, and psychosomatic illnesses are a few behaviors which can reveal the inner workings of the mind and body, and thus they become good end points upon which to concentrate stress reduction efforts. One of the most prevalent stress responses is muscle tension; excess muscle tension augments anxiety and is responsible for many psychosomatic illnesses.

Most experts in the relaxation field feel that reducing excess muscle tension not only directly reduces total body tension and anxiety but also indirectly helps eliminate the psychological forerunner of the muscle tension. It is no wonder that muscles are the one organ system which is included in almost every relaxation program; it is known that one cannot relax the mind or fully concentrate if the brain is being bombarded by muscle tension impulses. Whether muscle tension reduction is considered an end in itself or a means to an end, it is an essential step in this procedure.

It was mentioned in the introduction to this book that ultimate success depends upon compliance with the procedures and activities presented, and good educational theory suggests that compliance is enhanced by understanding what you are doing and why. So, rather than having you blindly jump in and follow, cookbook style, we will first present some basic information.

It was mentioned in the first chapter that your muscles are your only means of expression. All of your movements—running, fighting, smiling, crying, focusing your eyes, frowning, just to mention a few—can be achieved only through contraction of muscles. Even though the smooth muscles, also known as involuntary muscles, perform their function automatically, most of the body's musculature is voluntary and under direct mental control. Oddly enough, many of the orders are given subconsciously and many are counterproductive, contributing to excess body tension.

While the word "tension" is synonymous with muscle contraction, in the broad context of stress it usually means excess and inappropriate muscle contraction. A muscle is a mass of millions of cells which have the ability to contract, or to shorten, thus producing movement. As we learn how to perform activities, patterns of muscle movements are ingrained in our memory and become automatic functions. You do not have to think how to pick up a pencil, but rather just think of the act and the muscles respond. Other muscle action patterns are learned as well, such as striking out, running away, bracing for anticipated harm. When a threatening situation occurs, each muscle does not have to be commanded to act; you just think of the action, "run," and your legs move.

This concept is simple enough when the threatening situation is obvious. The muscles contract and the job gets done. However, in our modern, socially controlled world there are few physically threatening situations one must face during the average day. Most threats are symbolic and do not necessitate all-out action of fighting or running. But social forces and demands do cause anger and threaten egos, so subconsciously you prepare for action. This process is referred to as **alerting** or **bracing**. Muscles contract, but not enough to produce obvious movement. Thus, you do not get feedback as to the extent of the muscle activity. What results is an incomplete or partial contraction referred to as **muscle tension**. This tension is inappropriate, as no work is done and it serves no purpose. If the tension is prolonged, the muscles set up a learned pattern of response and chronically assume this state. Chronic, long-term tension has been related to numerous disorders, and because the origin of the muscle tension is in the defensive or alerting posture and attitude, these disorders are considered psychosomatic.

Take a moment and move your attention from this book to your body. First note your general overall position. Are you sitting comfortably? Is your body supported by the chair, or are you sitting in a way that strains your back muscles? Are your arms supported, or are you holding the book in the air? Are your fists clenched? Think back to times of writing reports. Have you ever noticed that you were holding the pen so tightly that it was leaving an indentation in your finger? Think of another activity, such as driving a car. Have you ever found yourself with a death grip on the steering wheel, producing tension up your arms to your shoulders, neck, back, and even to the head and face muscles?

These are examples of tension being exhibited through the muscles. More specifically, it is excess and needless muscle tension, as it is far in excess of what is needed to accomplish the task. This excess muscle tension is both a response to stress and a cause of stress. You can view stress as an expression of an internal state, and muscle action represents the outward expression of that state. The often-mentioned fight or flight syndrome is muscular expression, as are speech, facial expression, and eye movements.

Most movement are readily observable—that is, you can see the fingers move a pencil as one writes—but it takes a second look to notice if there is excess pressure. Excess exertion has nothing to do with writing. It is an outward expression of the anxiety or resentment over the work and/or it represents the general state of tension constantly with you. It is no mystery how individuals with experience at observing stress can quickly pick out stressed people by analyzing certain characteristics of their penmanship.

Much of the harmful, stress-producing muscle tension is extremely subtle and very difficult to detect. If you are thinking defensive thoughts, you start to assume a defensive posture. It is practially impossible to think of an action and not have your muscles prepare for the potential action. To illustrate this phenomenon, take out a pendant on a chain, or tie a key to a string and hold it out in front of you. Close your eyes, rest your elbow on a table, and without moving your hand, imagine the object swinging toward and away from you. After a few moments open your eyes: chances are it will be moving in that direction. Imagine it moving side to side, or circling, and those movements will also occur. Even though your hand did not actually move, the thought was translated to your fingers and tension developed in a rhythmical pattern with enough force to cause the object to move. This experiment shows that we have the ability to anticipate, which is necessary for preparation. Unfortunately, we often spend so much time in unproductive imagined preparation that our bodies adapt by increasing general muscle tension. At several points in this book we mentioned Selye's concept of disease of adaptation. Muscle tension represents a good example. The tense individual who is defensive and is constantly imagining action creates a situation in which the body becomes very efficient and adapts by maintaining a chronic state of muscle tension.

If such a condition is permitted to exist for an extended period of time, a wide variety of physical disorders may be produced or exaggerated. A few of the more common disorders are tension headaches, muscle cramps and spasms (such as writer's cramp), limitation of range of movement and flexibility, susceptibility to muscle injuries such as tears and sprains, insomnia, a wide variety of gastrointestinal maladies (constipation, diarrhea, colitis), renal system problems, dysmenorrhea. This list seems endless, but remember that the muscular system is involved in every body process and in every expression of emotion.

The connection between inordinate muscle tension and pathology was made hundreds of years ago, but it was not until the end of the last century that systematic relaxation programs were formulated. The names of Schultz, Sweigard, Maja Schade, and Jacobson became synonymous with relaxation training, as their pioneering work formed the basis of most of the relaxation programs in existence today. All of the techniques have the same basic objective of teaching the individual to relax the muscles at will by first developing an awareness of what it feels like to be tense and then what it feels like to be relaxed. If one is able to distinguish between tension and relaxation, control over tension follows almost effortlessly.

The relaxation program presented in this book is a matrix program made up of four parts which can be used in different combinations to accomplish distinctly different results. The four parts are 1) contraction–relaxation, 2) stretch–relaxation, 3) relaxation recall, and 4) freedom posturing.

Each cell in the matrix may be practiced alone or may be combined with the three other cells in the vertical column to accomplish specific goals (which will be outlined later) or each cell may be combined with the other cells on the horizontal plane to accomplish specific goals (which also will be discussed in greater detail). These exercises train the muscles, as well as the nervous system components that control muscle activity. The resultant reduction of tension in the muscles represents a significant reduction in total body tension. One will eventually develop an inherent self-awareness to the point that a little internal alarm goes off when tension starts to rise. Another benefit is mind control, which has been mentioned often throughout this book. To accomplish any of these techniques one must learn to focus on the task or problem and control the mind's tendency to wander.

The Matrix Relaxation Program

The purpose of the **contraction–relaxation** exercises is to develop an awareness of tension. In order to accomplish this, one must first sense the tension, and the most obvious way is to contract the muscle. This first contraction is followed by less intense contractions to the point where one can sense the minute tension of a resting muscle.

Sit back in your chair, close your eyes, and try to focus your thoughts on your muscles. Bend your arm up so that your hand touches your shoulder. The muscle tension is obvious as movement occurs. Relax. . . . Next, just think of that same movement. You almost have to hold the arm back as it seems to want to move. Feel the muscles contract ever so slightly. Try the same activity with your forehead. Frown, feeling the muscles contract. Relax. . . . This time just think of frowning and feel the tension develop. Relax. . . . Next, think of an activity that is unpleasant to you and try to feel the tension which may develop in the area that would be involved. You are, of course, getting feedback of subtle muscle activity which does not produce movement only because you have not willed the movement. But just as the gross movement can be controlled, so can the more subtle muscle tension if its existence is known.

The second phase of the Matrix Relaxation Program consists of **stretch-relaxation** exercises. The health benefits of the stretch-relaxation technique have been known for centuries; these exercises form the basis for Hatha Yoga programs, are an essential part of most calisthenic programs, and represent an innate pattern of movement. Notice your pet dog or cat, especially upon awakening, but other times during the day also. They never attempt to get up without first stretching. Humans also naturally go through a series of stretches before arising from sleep or after prolonged sitting. When tightness or tension is sensed, stretching is a natural reflex.

Our modern living patterns are directly responsible for a multitude of health problems, which have already been listed in earlier sections of the book. One of the most pervasive is shortened muscles, tendons, and ligaments. Our basic body structure and function have not changed since the days of the caveman, yet our daily activities have changed drastically. Since the body is adaptive, continual sitting during work and leisure will eventually result in shortened muscles, tendons, and ligaments which eventually result in restricted movements. It is not unusual for adults in their mid-twenties to be so restricted that touching their fingers to their toes while keeping the knees straight is impossible or at least very painful. The spine will condition itself to the state demanded by chronic sitting and lose its natural erect capabilities; the result will be a sitting type of posture while one is standing or walking. This posture naturally produces pain and tension as body parts are positioned unnaturally. Neck and facial muscles, tendons, and ligaments will pull unnaturally, producing pain which is sensed in the sensitive tissue around the head, and thus causing headache. It is not at all unusual for the posture and the tonus of the muscles under the skin to resemble those of the very old. "Age lines" are not a natural process of aging and are surely not natural in the young or even those in the middle years. Chronically shortened muscles do not function properly; excess tension and internal viscosity prohibit normal functioning, and a vicious cycle of the tension reflex develops. Gradually, movements become inefficient and labored; more energy than necessary is required and fatigue causes a chronic tired feeling even after adequate amounts of sleep. It has long been known that a muscle that has proper stretch capabilities is stronger, more efficient, and more enduring than one that is chronically shortened. Moreover, such a muscle is more contractible, it exhibits less residual tension, and it can be relaxed more easily.

It will be stated again and again during the exercise plan that your body will move when it is ready. This program is sequenced to condition natural readiness. **Do not** go beyond your point of pain or you will tear the tissue and retard your progress. You have spent many years conditioning this state and you cannot reverse it overnight. **Do not** set goals too high too fast. These are powerful exercises with the capability of restoring the natural structure and function to your tissues. Use them as directed until you have reconditioned your body.

The third phase of the Matrix Relaxation Program is **relaxation-recall** training. The mechanism underlying this technique is simply a conditioned pattern of responses which become associated with particular thoughts. Recall how thinking of yourself or your loved ones dying or being involved in a serious accident gives you chills or raises the hair on the back of your neck. This represents a conditioned physical response to that particular association. The opposite is just as true and produces an equally dramatic physical response. Imagine sitting on a quiet beach with the sun warming your body and a relaxation response is triggered. Unfortunately, many of us have become more conditioned to negative thoughts than to positive ones; thus the technique of relaxation was developed to help condition relaxation.

Relaxation recall is actually a very advanced form of relaxation training; it is learned more rapidly when the individual already possesses some other relaxation skills. For example, we have said many times that it is difficult to concentrate or control the direction of your thoughts if the mind is being bombarded by arousal impulses from your body. In each four-part exercise series the contraction-relaxation and stretch-relaxation phases set the stage for a more successful relaxation-recall response. The components of relaxation recall—concentration and relaxation—are facilitated by your ability to vividly imagine a scene or feeling state and by the ability to concentrate without arousal. Let's look at one of the techniques which is included in the exercise plan so you will better understand it when you are asked to perform it. It is known that one of the physical responses that accompanies relaxation is vasodilation, an expansion of the arteries in the skin of the extremities. This produces a warm, heavy sensation as blood flow increases in that area. Generally speaking, relaxed individuals tend to have warmer hands and anxious or stressed individuals tend to have cooler hands. If one can imagine warmth, or on a feeling level can reproduce the heavy sensation, the body has the tendency to "relive" or reproduce that state. A shift in blood flow is impossible without a change in nervous system tone; thus relaxation is facilitated. After a degree of proficiency has been obtained, we will add a more complex imagination process by utilizing personal visual imagery of a time and place that was particularly relaxing to you. If your "feeling memory" is pretty good and if you have developed some fair body control and concentration abilities, the memory of the beautiful times in your life can be one of your keys to controlling stress and tension.

We have said that stress arousal is a psychophysiological response to a particular psychosocial event. Each situation produces an immediate stress response, but also leaves a residual amount of tension in the body. Response to subsequent stressors is augmented by the residual left over from previous responses. As the day wears on, response overactivity results from the inability to dissipate residual tension. The physical relaxation produced by relaxation exercises is an immediate reaction, but the more the relaxation state is induced, the more the carry-over to times more removed from the exercise time. Gradually you experience a dissipation of residual tension. Thus each new stressful situation will produce a reaction sufficient to deal only with that particular situation without the add-on effect of previous stress arousal. The longer you practice the relaxation exercises, the more your general state of arousal resembles the relaxed state, and the ongoing tensions most detrimental to the body are greatly reduced. After a while, this relaxed state becomes a stable part of your personality. The overactive, rushed individual can become a slowed, cooler-reacting person who has the ability to respond with the intensity demanded of each situation as an isolated incident.

Chronically stressed and anxious people do not perceive internal states of arousal and do not associate physical states with emotional arousal. As in a positive feedback system, the physical arousal causes anxious feelings, which further cause physical arousal. Relaxation not only diminishes physical arousal, but promotes stress desensitization by allowing individuals to experience previously stressful situations in a relaxed state, gradually diminishing the stressful experience in their lives and reducing anxiety.

One essential to mental health, productivity, and happiness is the ability to live each current situation in reality without the effect of adding imaginary consequences of what could or should happen. Perhaps the primary therapeutic benefit of this relaxation program is the development of the ability to concentrate attention on the present, to quiet the imagination, and to distinguish reality from fantasy. You can develop the ability to direct thoughts away from the ego self, the primary source of stress, and direct it to the problem at hand. You can become more problem centered and less ego centered. As you become less stressed, you automatically become more efficient; they go hand in hand.

The fourth phase of the Matrix Relaxation Program consists of **freedom posturing** exercises which are designed to help you change thoughts and behaviors that continually fuel your stress furnace. Often the ways in which we process information and relate to others, especially at work, perpetuate the molehill-to-mountain phenomenon. We are too ready to allow ourselves to be frustrated, to be angered, to be disappointed or in general to be unhappy. We are too ready to hear and accentuate the negative instead of the positive. We "read into" others intentions that are not really there; we develop a pattern of thought which is stress-producing. This fourth phase will promote self-awareness and suggest ways of reducing such behavior especially as it relates to dealing with the expectations others have for you.

We will spend less time being uptight if we can recognize who, what, and, most important, when we are becoming stressed. You will recall that one of the underlying principles of biofeedback consisted of developing self-awareness to the point of being your own early warning system, sensing stressful arousal before it becomes too severe. Freedom posturing contains exercises which will help you to develop your autobiofeedback system, that is, to sense your biological state without instruments, by seeing yourself and others during stress.

After you have learned some of the powerful relaxation techniques, you then have to refine your use of them so as to be able to relax at will. Once you have developed the ability to relax at will, you can 1) practice and gradually condition your system to be more tranquil and relaxed and 2) use your ability to relax for immediate relief when you feel stressed. The catch in number 2 lies in our ability to recognize stress as it builds and before it pushes us into unproductive emotional states and physical disability. We will learn some autofeedback techniques in practicing the matrix exercises.

The Learning Phase

What follows is a detailed set of instructions on a 4-by-5 Matrix Relaxation Program. The learning phase necessitates more structured time involvement, more concentration, and more commitment than will be necessary once you master the techniques. Once you have perfected the techniques, you will be able to choose the particular exercise sequence which is most beneficial to you and which meets your immediate needs. As we have said many times, it is not our intention for you to practice a specific exercise, at a specific time for the rest of your life. You will know how, you will know why, and, in the final analysis, you will build your own individual program. However, it is very important that in the learning phase you follow the instructions and practice the exercises as suggested.

We have developed a technique which follows a natural patterning and which has proven over the years to be more effective and more easily learned than other relaxation techniques. The first two phases (contraction-relaxation and stretch-contraction) of each series consist of gross muscle actions which are innate to human movement and can be easily identified and controlled. These movements provide an excellent basis for learning as you gain awareness and conscious control over your muscle movements. Progression to higher levels of skilled activity can then be achieved.

Preparation for Exercise

In order for the learning experience to be as effective as possible, you should do whatever is possible to create an environment that enhances concentration. A few minutes spent in preparing the environment and the body will be a good investment. The first essential is a quiet environment, both external and internal. A quiet room away from others not participating is helpful, especially while you are learning. Put out the dog, cat, or whatever. Take the phone off the hook or have the calls stopped. Generally, do whatever can be done to reduce external noise. If you cannot completely eliminate the noise, as is often the case in busy households or offices, wear ear plugs or play a record or tape of soft instrumental sounds or use any of the numerous environmental sound recordings which are commercially available. Many enterprising individuals take their tape recorders to the woods to record the sound of the wind whistling through the trees, a mountain stream, or just the sounds of the birds at dawn. The sounds of the waves at the seashore also make an excellent background. Besides blocking out noise, such sounds help promote a sense of relaxation, as they usually bring back memories of pleasant feelings.

If the exercises are being done in a group setting, the room should be large enough so each participant can stretch out comfortably without feeling crowded. Body position will change with the exercises. Some necessitate lying down, some sitting or standing. Still others can be done in a variety of positions; for those, each individual will have to find his/her own preferred position. For lying down, a foam mat is helpful for reducing the pressure on body parts.

It is a good idea to place a note on the door to alert potential intruders that quiet is needed. However, it is advisable to assume a mental set that disturbances will happen. Expect them, deal with them, and do not allow them to make you angry or the emotion of the disturbance will linger long after the physical presence is gone. Of course, physical factors such as lighting, temperature, and ventilation should be optimal. Clothing should be comfortable. It is best to wear loose, soft clothes which you are not going to worry about wrinkling. If shoes, belts, bra, tie, or collar are too tight, loosen them. The goal is to diminish sensory input to the central nervous system. Most people like to have a clock where it can be seen at a glance to reduce the anxious feelings that arise through concern about the amount of time being spent.

In regard to the time of day that exercises should be performed, the fact is there is no best time for everyone. You will have to determine for yourself when and how long. Some programs dictate exactly how much time to spend and when to spend it. That's great if your life is very ordered. But chances are that your life is not that uniform. You are probably active, busy, involved with varying tasks and schedules. To limit your exercise to one specific time of the day would ritualize it, and if for some reason you could not exercise at that specific time, you would probably not do it at all that day. Also, there may be times you just don't feel up to it at that time. If you force yourself too much, you will do it halfheartedly and gain little from the experience. So find a convenient time: if it is the same time every day, fine; if not, that's fine also. The important thing is to engage in the program every day if at all possible. As to how much time to spend each session, again this will vary with your schedule. In the learning phase, try to complete an entire series at one time. After that, although it is still preferable to complete an entire series, it is better to work for a few minutes here and there than not at all. You will be surprised how much waiting time you have during the day which could be utilized for exercises, especially the quiet relaxation series. When you are waiting for a meeting to start or an appointment to arrive, or waiting for a bus or even waiting for one of these seemingly eternal stoplights to change—5 minutes here and there can add up quickly and you might just find yourself much less perturbed about being kept waiting. You can think of it as time for yourself and for your self-improvement.

How to Use the Matrix Relaxation Program

The matrix plan consists of five vertical columns and four horizontal rows containing independent sets of relaxation exercises. The vertical columns contain exercises which correspond to sections of the body: A) the chest and breathing process, B) the lower extremities, C) the trunk, D) the upper extremities, and E) the head, neck, and face. The exercises in the horizontal rows correspond to the four types of exercises representing the four parts of the program: 1) contraction–relaxation, 2) stretch–relaxation, 3) relaxation recall, and 4) freedom posturing exercises. Thus, each of the vertical columns contains four cells which are sequenced so each cell will prepare you for the next exercise cell; this pattern allows for a steady, rapid progression toward a **deep state of relaxation**. The horizontal rows contain five cells each, each row utilizing a specific technique that is practiced briefly with each section of the body, thus promoting **total body relaxation**. Whether you use the horizontal or vertical program, you will more readily obtain maximal benefits if you complete all of the exercises in the respective row or column at one time, especially while learning. After that you will become experienced enough to use cells independently or mix them in a manner you find successful. For example:

1. Generally speaking, if you are usually nervous or fidgety and have difficulty relaxing, you will probably find Row 1 or Row 2 best to start your relaxation program. On the other hand, if you have a good imagination and have no difficulty in sitting still, you may find Row 3 or Row 4 best for total body relaxation.
2. If you need more practice on correct diaphragmatic breathing, complete cells A1 and A2.
3. If your job requires long hours of standing or sitting, complete cells B1 and B2.
4. If you have posture problems, complete cells C1 and C2.
5. If you write or type all day, complete cells D1 and D2.
6. If you are bothered by tension headache, complete entire Column E.
7. If you have extreme difficulty sitting still and concentrating, complete all of Row 1 and/or entire Row 2.

8. If you need to increase powers of concentration, complete Rows 3 and 4.
9. If you lack space or privacy to do physical movements, complete Rows 3 and 4.
10. If you have breathing problems or are short of breath, complete all of Column A.
11. If you are troubled by varicose veins, complete all of Column B.
12. If you have "psychosomatic lower back pain," complete Column C.
13. If you suffer bruxism (teeth grinding or clenching), complete cell E1.
14. If you have only 10 minutes and you really need to calm down, complete cells A1 and E3.
15. If you wish to increase your powers of imagination and creativity, complete cell E3 and all of Row 4.
16. If you are in the middle of a stressful situation, complete cells A1, A2, A3 and/or E3.
17. If you have difficulty falling asleep at night, begin by completing Column A and then complete Row 1.
18. If you want to increase your powers of self and body awareness, complete all of Row 4.
19. If you want to center on possible sources of your stress, complete all of Row 4.

To summarize: you will notice that the intent of completing each of the vertical columns is to progressively deepen your level of relaxation for a specific area of your body. The intent of completing each of the respective horizontal rows is to provide you with a choice of four different strategies for gaining total body relaxation.

You may do more than one set of exercises at one time, but be careful you do not tire and get sloppy in your procedure. Full attainment of desired results requires your full concentration. The most common mistake people make is to rush through relaxation. It would be most beneficial, especially while you are learning the exercises, to practice every day. After that it still would be best to practice every day, but we are confident that by that time you will learn to listen to your body's needs and your success will provide your motivation.

The objectives are success in:
1. Immediate reduction of situational tension
2. Long-term control of excess stress and tension
3. Increased powers of concentration
4. Increased powers of imagination and creativity
5. Getting a good night's sleep.

The exercises in the relaxation matrix are easy to do. They require no prior knowledge or physical conditioning. They can be

THE MATRIX RELAXATION PROGRAM

	Column A Breathing	Column B Lower Extremities	Column C Trunk	Column D Upper Extremities	Column E Head, Neck, Face	
ROW 1 Contraction–Relaxation	A1 Breathing down Time: 1 min	B1 Gas pedal exercises Time: 3 min	C1 Arch back Flat back Time: 2 min	D1 Extend and reach Flex and pull Time: 2 min	E1 Head rotation Teeth clenching Time: 3 min	ROW 1 TOTAL TIME: 11 min
ROW 2 Stretch–Relaxation	A2 Controlled tempo breathing Time: 4 min	B2 Toe raise Knee stretch Toe touch Time: 2 min	C2 Back stretch, forward/back Trunk bend Time: 2 min	D2 Wall reach Sky reach Shoulder roll Back reach Shoulder elevation Time: 3 min	E2 Neck stretches Forced stretch Head roll Time: 4 min	ROW 2 TOTAL TIME: 15 min
ROW 3 Relaxation Recall	A3 Breath counting Time: 10 min	B3 Legs heavy and warm Time: 5 min	C3 Center of warmth Time: 5 min	D3 Arms heavy and warm Time: 5 min	E3 Your special place Time: 8 min	ROW 3 TOTAL TIME: 33 min
ROW 4 Freedom Posturing	A4 Breathing easily Time: 5 min	B4 Legs loose and light Time: 5 min	C4 Unlocking your trunk Time: 5 min	D4 Relaxing your grip Time: 5 min	E4 Removing your mask Time: 5 min	ROW 4 TOTAL TIME: 25 min
TOTAL TIME OF COLUMNS	20 min	15 min	14 min	15 min	20 min	

When attempting the stretching or contraction exercises, extend yourself only as far as you can comfortably. Do not concern yourself with completing them exactly as described when first learning. As your skill level increases, attempt to come as close as you can to performing the exercises as described.

completed in a short period of time each day, which is a small investment for large dividends of increased health and happiness.

The rest of this chapter explains the specific exercises in the Matrix Relaxation Program. Read each set of instructions thoroughly before attempting any of the exercises.

Breathing

Wouldn't you know it! The first thing in life we learned to do, and we learned it wrong. We are referring here to the act of breathing. But, you say, breathing is a natural, automatic body function; how can breathing be right or wrong? You should realize by now that any body process can be altered and, if the practice is prolonged, can be conditioned. For reasons too numerous and involved to discuss here, most of us have developed and conditioned inefficient and improper breathing techniques. And what could be more important than bringing in fresh air and revitalizing the body tissues. Ancient yoga philosophy states that mind is the master of the senses and breath is the master of the mind, and that breathing is the elixir of life.

Actually, the exchange of air is only one aspect of breathing important to the relaxation process. Breathing is an involuntary, automatic function which reflects our general state of stress arousal. But breathing is also voluntary and can be manipulated. If we so desire, we can breathe fast or slow, our inhalations can be deep or shallow, our expirations can be partial or complete, and in some cases we even "choose" difficult or pathological breathing patterns. By learning to breathe correctly, we take in air more efficiently, the pulmonary system is strengthened and conditioned, the function of the cardiovascular system is enhanced, greater oxygenation is promoted, the nerves are calmed, and restfulness occurs. The breathing centers in the brain have a facilitating relationship with the arousal centers; therefore, constant, steady, restful breathing promotes relaxation. It is almost impossible to be tense and have slow, relaxed, deep breaths, so control breathing and you control tension. Condition breathing and you condition your system to be more tranquil. The power of deep, steady breathing is instinctual. When you want to control your energy—when lifting a heavy object, for example—you instinctively hold your breath. When you want to center yourself—when pulling the string of a bow or the trigger of a gun, for instance—you instinctively breathe deep and hold. It is your most natural way of centering yourself or concentrating.

The practicing of breathing techniques not only facilitates relaxation, but plays a vital role in prevention of respiratory ailments. Individuals with respiratory disorders like asthma and emphysema can benefit not only from increased oxygenation, but also from learning correct, efficient, and less stressful breathing patterns. But even for those of us without respiratory system pathology, breathing is often labored and inefficient. At rest we normally use only one third of our lung capacity. Through breathing exercises, you will be able to vitalize these functions, regulate breathing patterns, build up respiratory reserve, and increase oxygenation capacity.

In correct breathing the floating ribs (lower five pairs) are moved by the intercostal muscles between the ribs and the diaphragm as it lowers toward the abdomen. This movement allows for expansion of the lower lobes of the lungs, creating a vacuum, and the air rushes in. If you keep the abdominal muscles tight during the breathing movement, your diaphragm cannot descend and the lower lobes cannot fill, so a deep breath is possible only by a hyperexpansion of the top lobes, and this method expends much more energy. Many of us have developed the habit of high breathing because it is thought to represent a more "masculine" posture—stomach in, chest out. This is not to say that one should not have strong, taut stomach muscles. On the contrary, contraction–relaxation movements will further strengthen stomach muscles without a chronic shortening developing. It is also important not to neglect exhalation. You must deeply exhale to get the stale used air out or there is less room for fresh air to enter. Generally, exhalation lasts longer than inhalation. Correct breathing, once mastered, becomes a chronic exercise which expands and contracts the lung tissue, developing strength and endurance.

Learning to Breathe

Learning more efficient breathing patterns can be facilitated by the ability to perform the following exercises and differentiate between them.

1. Upper costal breathing.

Use your hands to sense the action of the respiratory movements. Place your hands on the upper one third of the chest wall, preferably crossing the hands with the fingertips resting comfortably over the collarbone. You can easily sense the expansion of the upper lobes of the lungs with your fingertips in the open space between the collarbone and the trapezius muscle which runs behind that bone. Keeping your abdominal wall relaxed, inhale through your nose, expanding the upper ends of your lungs as fully as possible. Hold your breath for 3 seconds, then let go, exhaling slowly, letting the air gently flow from the mouth. Repeat this exercise five times, resting for five normal breaths between each one. The pause in between is important, as you want to avoid hyperventilation and allow yourself time to center your thoughts on the activity and reflect on what was sensed or felt.

2. Middle costal breathing.

Again, let your fingers be your sensors. Place your fingers on the middle one third of the chest wall below the nipples (sixth rib). Keeping your abdominal and upper costal area relaxed, inhale through your nose, expanding the mid-chest region as fully as possible. Hold for 3 seconds and gently exhale through the mouth. Repeat this five times and then relax quietly. Remember to pause between each repetition.

3. Diaphragmatic breathing.

Breathing with the diaphragm is performed by taking a deep inspiration with the belly pushed down and out by the movement of the diaphragm, thus allowing the lower lobes of the lungs to inflate fully. Your hands are placed on the lower ribs, where they should easily sense the breathing motion. With the upper chest relaxed, inhale deeply. The abdominal wall is pushed up and out. Hold for 3 seconds and exhale, feeling the abdominal wall descend toward the spine. Repeat this exercise five times. Diaphragmatic breathing stretches the lower lobes of the lungs, thus allowing more fresh air to enter. It also acts to correct shallow breathing habits, allowing increased depth of inspiration.

4. Very deep breathing.

Start by exhaling every bit of air from your lungs. Force the air out, and feel the space between your belly and spine shrink. When all the air is out, inhale slowly, using the diaphragmatic technique. Picture your lungs as a glass being filled with water—bottom, middle, then top. Hold your breath for 3 seconds and then exhale gently through your nose or mouth. It sounds as though we are asking for an exaggerated, strenuous action, but we are not. Breathe from your diaphragm, naturally and effortlessly. Concentrate on the air traveling through the air passageways. With each expiration feel a sense of increased relaxation. Feel a sense of letting go. Begin to feel the looseness in your body, an uncoiling feeling as you settle down and pull your mind and body together. Repeat this exercise five times, resting between each repetition.

Now that you know how to breathe correctly, go on to the Column A exercises on breathing. You may periodically want to repeat these learning-to-breathe exercises until you feel that you have them fully mastered. Once you do, just start with the Column A exercises on breathing.

Column A: Breathing Exercises

Exercise A1. Breathing Down

During the course of an average day, many of us find ourselves in anxiety-producing situations. Our heart rates increase, our stomachs may become upset, and our thoughts may race uncontrollably through our minds. In such moments we tend to make poor decisions or just overreact. It is during such episodes as these that we require fast-acting relief from our stressful reactions so we can calmly attempt to solve the crisis or problem at hand. The brief exercise described below has been found effective for quickly calming down in stressful situations.

The basic mechanism for stress reduction in this exercise involves deep breathing. The procedure is as follows:

Step 1. Assume a comfortable position. Rest your left hand (palm down) on top of your abdomen. More specifically, place your left hand over your navel. Now place your right hand so that it comfortably rests on your left. Your eyes should remain open. (See Fig. 12.1)

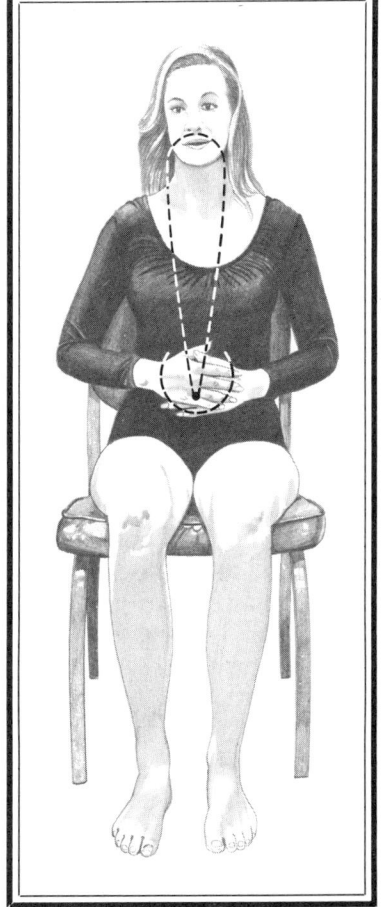

Fig. 12.1

Step 2. Imagine a hollow bottle, or pouch, lying internally beneath the point at which your hands are resting. Begin to inhale. As you inhale imagine that the air is entering through your nose and descending to fill that internal pouch. You hands will rise as you fill the pouch with air. As you continue to inhale, imagine the pouch being filled to the top. Your rib cage and upper chest will continue the wave-like rise that was begun at your navel. The total length of your inhalation should be 3 seconds for the first week or so, then lengthening to 4 or 5 seconds as you progress in skill development. Remember to concentrate on "seeing" the air move as you inhale and exhale.

Step 3. Hold your breath. Keep the air inside the pouch. Repeat to yourself the phrase "My body is calm."

Step 4. Slowly begin to exhale—to empty the pouch. As you do, repeat to yourself the phrase "My body is quiet." As you exhale you will feel your raised abdomen and chest recede.

Repeat this 4-step exercise 4 to 5 times in succession. Should you begin to feel light-headed, stop at that point. If lightheadedness remains a problem, consider shortening the length of the inhalation and/or decreasing the total number of repetitions of the 4-step exercise.

Practice this exercise 10 to 15 times a day. Make it a ritual in the morning, afternoon, and evening, as well as during stressful situations. After a week or two of practice, omit Step 1. This was for teaching the technique only. Because this form of relaxation is a skill, it is important to practice at least 10 to 15 times a day. At first you may not notice any on-the-spot relaxation. However, after a week or two of regular practice you **will** increase your capabilities to relax on the spot. Remember—you must practice **regularly** if you are to master this skill. Regular, consistent practice of these daily exercises will lead to the development of a more calm and relaxed attitude—a sort of antistress attitude—and when you do have stressful moments, they will be far less severe.

Now continue with exercise A2.

Exercise A2. Controlled Tempo Breathing

This exercise develops powers of concentration, facilitates centering, and helps breath control. You may sit or lie down. Keep your eyes closed. The breathing will be diaphragmatic—quiet, natural and effortless. Concentrate on your breathing. Become part of it. With one hand, find your pulse in the wrist of the other arm. Count your pulse for one minute. While still counting your pulse, bring part of your attention back to your breathing. Count the number of pulses it takes you to make a normal inspiration, then how many to make a normal expiration. Do this several times until you have a rhythm. The average will be somewhere between five and ten. As an example, say the number is five. Still monitoring your pulse, breathe in with five beats of your pulse, hold for five, exhale for five, and remain quiet for five. Continue this for 3 minutes and then sit quietly and prepare for Exercise A3. At first you will tend to lose count, but as your powers of concentration increase, you will make it all the way. You can then increase the time spent doing this exercise.

Exercise A3. Breath Counting

This is another exercise to promote relaxation and increase powers of concentration. It is also used as a preparation for Exercise A4. You may do this sitting or lying down. As in Exercise A2, we will use quiet, normal diaphragmatic breathing. Concentrate on your breathing. As you breathe in, think "in." Let the air out and think "out." Think . . . in . . . out . . . in . . . out. Now each time you breathe out, count the breaths. Count ten consecutive breaths without missing a count. If you happen to miss one, start over. When you get to ten, start at one again. Do this ten times and then sit quietly and prepare for Exercise A4. Concentrate, anticipate the breath, block all other thoughts from your mind.

Exercise A4. Breathing Easily

If working with another person, just sit back and have him or her read the directions. If you are working by yourself, read the situation, get the idea of what you are being asked to do, then sit back, close your eyes, and work through it. Either way, always close your eyes because it **greatly** increases your power of concentration.

Situation 1.

Close your eyes, but in your mind's eye see a tense person. It may be someone you know well or just someone you have seen once. What does this person look like when he/she is stressed? How is that person sitting? What is (s)he doing with his/her legs, arms, face? Concentrate on his/her breathing: is the person breathing fast or slow, deep or shallow, through nose or mouth? What sounds is the person making?

Now, assume that position yourself. Breathe the way you see the imagined person breathing. See yourself in that position. Feel yourself in that position. Where are you? Who are you with? What message (verbal or nonverbal-implied) is the person giving to you? What is he/she expecting from you? Are you feeling pushed to do something you do not want to do? Or are you feeling held back from doing something you want to do? Now leave those thoughts, go and rest for a moment.

Situation 2.

Close your eyes and switch your mind's eye to a person whom you see as being very relaxed. How is he or she sitting? Concentrate on his/her breathing; how is it different from that of the tense person? Assume that position yourself. Breathe the way you see this relaxed person breathing. Where are you? Who are you with? Do you feel free to do what you want to do? In the absence of expectations this is how your body feels. You can help yourself demand your personal freedom by telling your body to breathe in this free manner. Now slowly open your eyes and reorient yourself to the world around you. Feel the energy flowing through your system vitalizing your sense of commitment to your purpose and to yourself. When you feel someone is pushing you or holding you back, assume this freedom posture and be aware of how you are more willing to demand your personal freedom.

Column B: The Lower Extremities

Column B exercises will focus on the very large muscle mass of the lower extremities. If muscles are capable of storing residual muscle tension, and they are, then the extremely large muscle mass of the legs represents a large depot. The legs are made to move. If you sit or even stand in a stationary position most of the day, chances are your leg muscles are being conditioned to remain in a partial state of contraction, storing residual tension. These exercises will not only help reduce tension immediately, they also provide a learning program which teaches voluntary control over muscle tension. Again, we progress from two different kinds of movement-relaxation exercises to quiet-relaxation exercises.

Exercise B1. Gas Pedal Exercises

The first exercise will involve only the **ankle joints**. This activity can be performed while you are sitting or lying down, although the latter position is preferred. The action will be to pull the foot toward the front of the leg (the movement involved in taking your foot off the gas pedal). The tension force is felt only in the muscles on the front and outside of the lower leg, not in the calf muscle. Doing both feet at once, pull your toes toward your legs as hard as possible until you feel uncomfortable (short of pain—if pain develops, rest for a moment and proceed less vigorously). Center your thoughts in the muscles experiencing the tension. Try to visualize the tension. Form an image in your mind about this tightness. Hold for a few seconds and let go. Repeat the exercise, being sure to synchronize your breathing. Breathe in, while pulling the feet up, then hold your breath while holding the contraction—let the air out and relax the muscles. Lie quietly for one minute, then repeat. (Fig. 12.2)

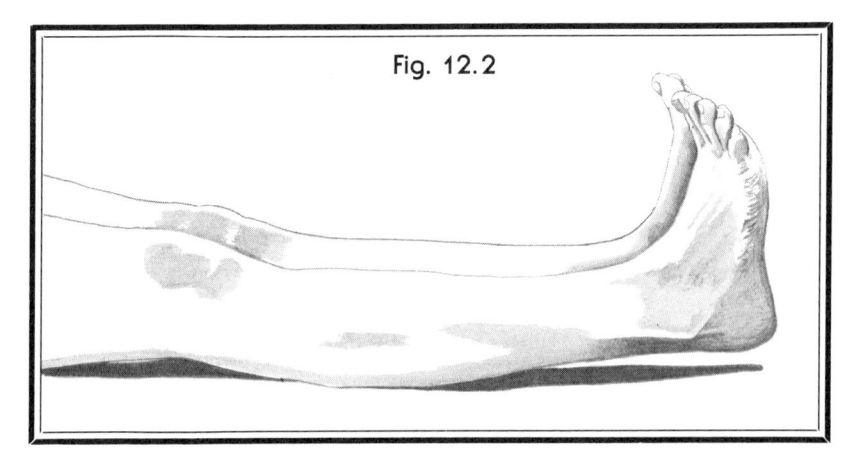

Fig. 12.2

After you have done this several times and feel comfortable with the activity and the breathing pattern, turn your awareness more toward the relaxation than the contraction. As you breathe out and relax, allow the muscles to go limp. As you pass over the peak of the contraction, begin to unwind. Try to form a visual image of this relaxed state and hold it in your mind. Repeat this exercise until you have gained confidence in your ability to relax these muscles.

Now move on to the **calf muscles**. These are the exact opposite of the first group; hence tightness will be felt in the calf area and the stretching sensation will be felt in the muscle group in the front of the lower leg. The action will be pointing your toes as in pushing down on the gas pedal. Keep the heels down. Start by taking a deep breath, pushing your toes down and away from the body as far as possible. When you reach the peak of your breath, hold the breath for 5 seconds, holding your toes in the pointed position. Now, slowly exhale while allowing the feet to come back to a resting position. (Fig. 12.3.)

Repeat this exercise three to five times, attempting to synchronize your breathing with the contraction and relaxation phases. As you exhale and let go of the contraction, form a visual image of the tension in the calf muscle flowing out with the air from your lungs. Feel an unwinding or letting go. Concentrate on the feelings of tension, the feelings of relaxation, and the difference between the two feelings.

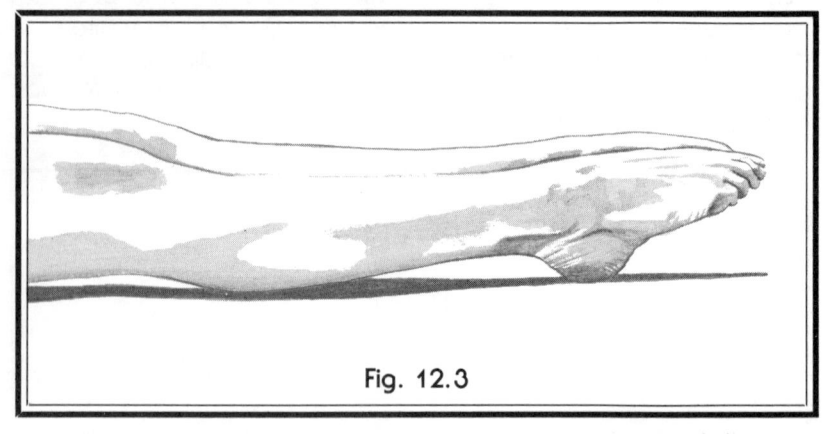

Fig. 12.3

The best exercise in this group is the extension of **the knee and hip** through pushing the knees down into the floor while keeping the legs straight. The tightness will be felt in the front of the thigh and in the buttocks area. No appreciable stretching force is perceived, because of the fact that these muscles are long and serve more than one joint. As always, begin with a deep breath, push your hips and knees down into the mat as hard as possible, heels off the floor. Hold at the peak of your breath, then exhale while allowing the muscles to rest. Again form an image of tension, feel the letting go. Repeat three to five times. (Fig. 12.4.)

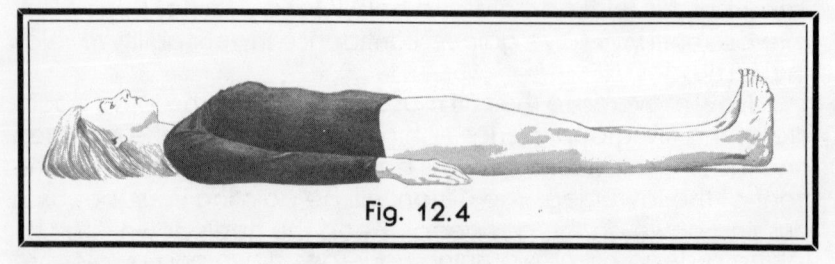

Fig. 12.4

Put these together in three successive movements, allowing about 30 seconds between each exercise. Lie quietly and relax.

Exercise B2. Toe Raise; Knee Stretch; Toe Touch

Even though muscles will contract during these positions, the emphasis is on stretch of muscles and joints. The first exercise is a simple **toe raise.** In a standing position with hands on hips or raised in front of you, balance yourself as high on the tips of your toes as possible. Hold for the count of 10 and relax. Repeat this exercise five times and relax. (Fig. 12.5.)

The second exercise is the **knee stretch.** Sit with your legs folded under you so that your buttocks are resting on your ankles. Your toes should be pointed backward. Place your hands on the floor outside and behind your feet. Straighten your body with head raised high. Hold for a count of ten; relax and repeat five times. (Fig. 12.6.)

The third exercise, the **toe touch,** stretches the muscles in the back of the leg in three positions. In a standing position with the heels together, toes angled slightly outward and legs straight, bend forward from the waist and place your hands on your knees. Hold for a count of ten and return to standing. If this produced no pain, the second repetition should find you reaching for your ankles. If pain was experienced, repeat the position to your knees. Don't force it; your body will tell you when it is ready to go lower. Hold for a count of ten and return to standing. On the third repetition,

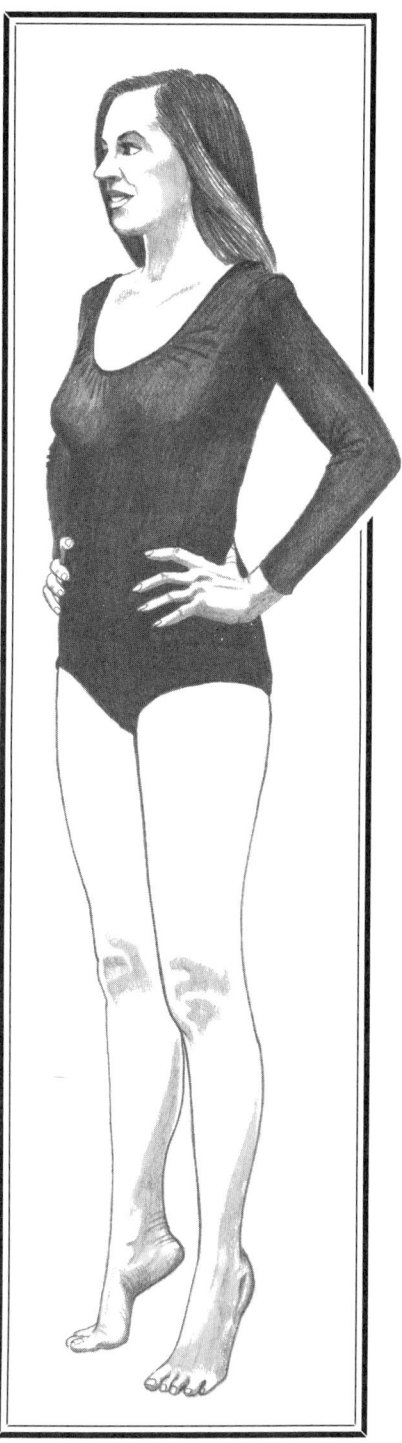

Fig. 12.5

128 THE STRESS MESS SOLUTION

Fig. 12.6

place the tips of your fingers on the floor, but assume this position only if no pain was experienced during the last one. Hold for ten and return to standing. The final position, assuming no pain to this point, is to place your palms flat on the floor. Keep your legs straight, bend at the waist, and hold for a count of ten. You will do four repetitions whether you reach the floor or not. Remember, go slowly; your body will tell you when to go on to the next position. (Fig. 12.7.)

Exercise B3. Legs Heavy and Warm

The exercises in this group are quiet concentration activities

Fig. 12.7

which can be done either sitting or lying down. The object is to tell yourself to reproduce feelings of heaviness and warmth in the legs. If you are successful, a heavy, warm sensation will occur as blood flow increases in that area. The body will "relive" or reproduce that state and, as we have said, such a shift is impossible without a change in nervous system tone. Thus relaxation is facilitated. You must be quiet and undistracted. You must concentrate.

Start by taking three deep breaths. Repeat the following phrases quietly to yourself: "I am relaxed. I am calm. I am quiet." Go slowly; allow time between each phrase to feel the sensations:

My right leg is heavy.
My right leg is heavy and warm.
My right leg is warm and relaxed.
I am calm and quite relaxed.
My left leg is heavy.
My left leg is heavy and warm.
My left leg is warm and relaxed.
I am calm and quite relaxed.
I am quiet and at peace.
I am relaxed.

This activity should take about 5 minutes. When you are done, remain quiet and flow directly into Exercise B4.

Exercise B4. Legs Loose and Light

If working with another person, just sit back and have him/her read the directions. If you are working by yourself, read the situation, get the idea of what you are being asked to do, then sit back, close your eyes, and work through it. Either way, always close your eyes because it greatly increases your powers of concentration.

Situation 1.

Close your eyes, but in your mind's eye, see a tense person. It may be someone you know well or just someone you have seen once. What does this person look like when he/she is stressed? What is the person doing with his/her legs . . . arms . . . face? Concentrate on the legs. Are they moving or still, crossed or open? Are feet flat on the floor? Do they seem to be digging into the floor as if to resist movement or just the opposite to provide a firm base from which to spring? Are the legs generally taut, ready for action?

Now assume that position yourself. Place your legs as you see the imagined person doing. Tense your muscles as the person tensed their muscles. See yourself in that position. Feel yourself in that position. Where are you? Who are you with? What message (verbal or nonverbal-implied) is the person giving to you? What is he/she expecting from you? Are you feeling pushed to do something you do not want to do? Or are you feeling held back from doing something you want to do? Now leave those thoughts and rest for a moment.

Situation 2.

Close your eyes and switch your mind's eye to a person whom you see as being very relaxed. How is this person sitting? Concentrate on his/her legs. How are they different from those of the tense person? Assume that position yourself. Where are you? Who are you with? Do you feel free to do what you want to do? In the absence of expectations this is how your body feels. You can help yourself demand your personal freedom by telling your body to position itself in this fashion. Now slowly open your eyes and reorient yourself to the world around you. Feel the energy flowing through your system vitalizing your sense of commitment to your purpose and to yourself. When you feel someone is pushing you or holding you back, assume this freedom posture and be aware of how you are more willing to demand your personal freedom.

Column C: The Trunk

Column C will focus on the muscles of the trunk. These muscles are perhaps the most abused by our modern sedentary lifestyle. Poor posture, low back pain, chronically shortened back muscles, and weak abdominal muscles plague almost every adult. Be particularly careful with the exercises in this series. Do not go beyond pain. You cannot undo years of abuse in one day. Your body will let you know when you can hold a position longer or advance to a more extreme position.

Exercise C1. Arch Back; Flat Back

We have chosen two exercises for this area. The first utilizes the extensor muscles of the lower back. This **arch back** exercise is particularly good for individuals with complaints of lower back discomforts not related to deformity or injury. As a large proportion of our population suffers from tension-related low back pain, we will repeat an earlier warning. If this or any of these exercises produces pain or spasms, stop the exercise and rest. Continue with less than maximal contraction, gradually increasing the strength of contraction over several weeks. The action in this exercise is hollowing or arching the back while lying on your back. The chest is moved slightly toward the chin. The pelvis is fixed on the floor. The tension is felt in the lower back area. Synchronize with your breathing, inhaling as you tense the muscles and exhaling as you relax; concentrate on the feelings of tension and relaxation. Hold for five counts, then exhale and relax. Repeat five times. (Fig. 12.8.)

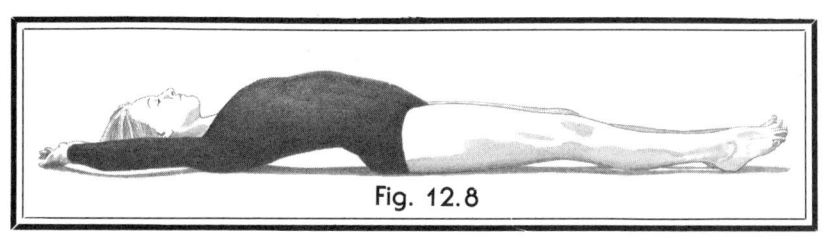

Fig. 12.8

The second exercise, **flat back**, is pulling in the abdominal muscles. Keep the legs, pelvis, and shoulders in contact with the floor. Breathe in, contract the stomach muscles, flatten the lower back against the floor, hold for five counts, then exhale and relax. Repeat five times. (Fig. 12.9.)

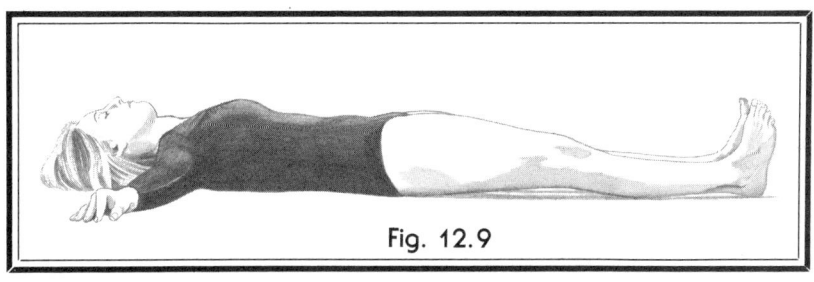

Fig. 12.9

Try them both, one after the other with 5-second rest intervals between them. Repeat five times. Concentrate on the feelings of tension and relaxation. The visual imagery is just as important as is the performance of the muscular exercise.

Exercise C2. Back Stretch Forward/Back; Trunk Bend

Here again, the emphasis is on the stretch of the muscle, the recoil, and the sense of relaxation which follows. Concentrate on the "afterfeeling" of extreme relaxation. The stretch relieves the partial contraction and allows the muscle to relax fully.

The first exercise is the **back stretch forward**. As its name implies, you will feel the stretch in different parts of your back as the exercise advances. Lie on the floor. Slowly tensing your stomach muscles, raise your trunk through the sitting position to a point where your head is as close to your knees as possible. Once there, place your hands on your knees, thumb on the inside of your leg, elbow held as high as possible. Hold for ten counts and return to the lying position. Move very slowly. Feel the stomach muscles contract as they raise and lower your upper body. Feel the stretch in the lower back. (Fig. 12.10.)

On the second repetition, place your hands halfway between your knees and ankles. Try to get your head to your knees; however, go only as far as your flexibility allows. Don't force it—you will get there one day soon. Hold for a count of ten and relax back to the lying position. Feel the stretch and subsequent relaxation in the back slightly higher than in repetition one.

On the third repetition, try for your ankles. Go slowly, feel the stretch a little higher on the back. Try to get your head to your knees. Hold for a count of ten and relax. For the fourth repetition, try to place your hands on the bottoms of your feet. Draw the trunk toward your legs. Allow your elbows to rest on the floor. Hold for a count of ten and slowly return to the lying position. Relax, feeling the tension release.

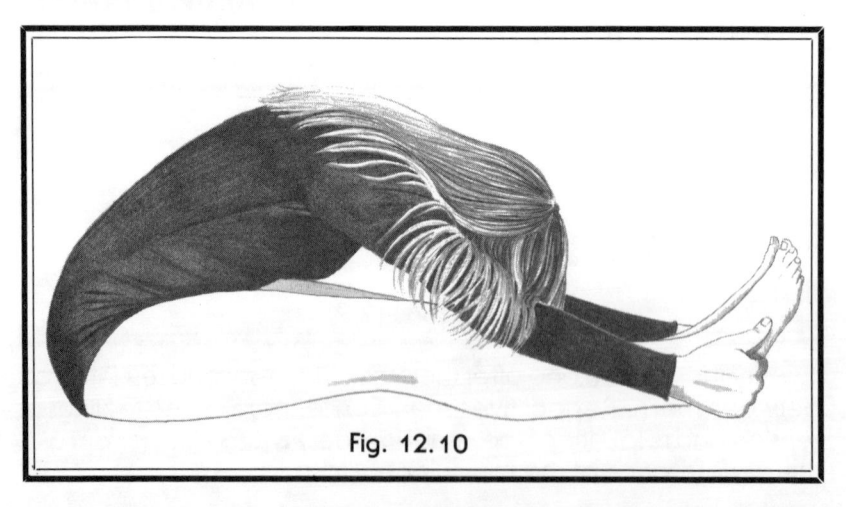

Fig. 12.10

For the second exercise, the **back stretch reverse**, you will need to lie down on your stomach. This exercise will stretch the back in the opposite direction. You will feel it in both the back and stomach. Place your hands, palms down on the floor, one on each side of your face. Slowly raise your upper body until you can rest your elbows on the floor. Hold in this position for a count of ten. If this produces no pain, arch your back slowly, moving your head high and back. Hold this position for a count of ten and rest. If this produces no pain, place your palms on the floor and continue to raise your upper body until your arms are straight. Go very slowly, and, if you feel pain, return to the last position. Hold for a count of ten and return to the floor and relax. Feel the tension release in the back and stomach. Relax and breathe softly. Repeat the entire sequence five times. (Fig. 12.11.)

Fig. 12.11

The third exercise is the **standing trunk bend.** Stand with your feet together, legs straight. The first motion will be a side bend. Stretch your arms over your head. Bend your trunk to the right. Go as far as possible. Try to achieve a right angle to your lower body. Go only as far as you can, and when there, hold for a count of ten and return to an erect position. Now repeat to the left. Hold for ten and return. Next, bend backward as far as you can. Hold for a ten count and return. The final move is forward. Bend to a right angle, hold for ten, and return. Move very slowly, feeling the stretch and the contraction. When you have done all four moves, bring your arms down to your side, and relax. Sense the feeling of relaxation. Repeat the entire sequence five times. (Figs. 12.12 through 12.14.)

Exercise C3. Center of Warmth

The exercises in this group are quiet concentration activities which may be done in the sitting or lying position. You will need quiet, intense concentration on the trunk area of the body. You are going to try to imagine warmth being emitted from the nerve plexis which lies behind the stomach right above the navel. Focus your attention on what you feel is the exact center of your body. The nerves there form a plexis called the **solar plexis.** Softly, slowly, and quietly say to yourself:

I am relaxed.
I am calm.
I am quiet.
My solar plexis is warm.
I can feel the heat radiating throughout my entire body.
My body is warm and relaxed.
I am quiet and at peace.
I am relaxed.

This activity should take about 5 minutes. When you are finished, remain quiet and flow directly into Exercise C4.

Fig. 12.12

Exercise C4. Unlocking Your Trunk

If working with another person, just sit back and have him or her read the directions. If you are working by yourself read the situation, get the idea of what you are being asked to do, then sit back, close your eyes, and work through it. Either way, always close your eyes because it greatly increases your powers of concentration.

Situation 1.

Close your eyes, but in your mind's eye see a tense person. It may be someone you know well or just someone you have seen

THE MATRIX RELAXATION PROGRAM   135

Fig. 12.13

once. What does this person look like when he/she is stressed? What is the person doing with his/her legs . . . arms . . . face? Concentrate on the midsection of the person's body. Is this person hunched over from the shoulders? Bent in the abdomen? Is the back arched? Or is the back being pushed into the chair?

Now assume that position yourself. Place your trunk as you see the imagined person doing. Tense your muscles as the person tensed the muscles. See yourself in that position. Feel yourself in that position. Where are you? Who are you with? What message (verbal or nonverbal-implied) is the person giving to you? What is he/she expecting from you? Are you feeling pushed to do something you do not want to do? Or are you feeling held back from

Fig. 12.14

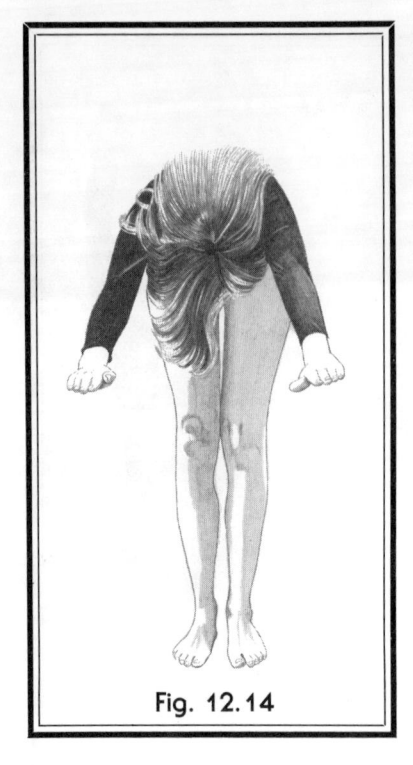

doing something you want to do? Now leave those thoughts and rest for a moment.

Situation 2.

Close your eyes and switch your mind's eye to a person whom you see as being very relaxed. How is this person sitting? Concentrate on his/her trunk. How is this different from that of the tense person? Assume the relaxed position yourself. Where are you? Who are you with? Do you feel free to do what you want to do? In the absence of expectations this is how your body feels. You can help yourself demand your personal freedom by telling your body to position itself in this fashion. Now slowly open your eyes and reorient yourself to the world around you. Feel the energy flowing through your system vitalizing your sense of commitment to your purpose and to yourself. When you feel someone is pushing you or holding you back, assume this freedom posture and be aware of how you are more willing to demand your personal freedom.

Column D: The Upper Extremities

This group of exercises concentrates on the fingers, arms, and shoulders. If you write or type most of the day, you will experience a great deal of tension in your arms and shoulders, and these exercises will act to relieve the residual tension built up by those activities. These exercises produce instant results and perhaps more than any of the others should be practiced for a short period of time on each break.

Exercise D1. Extend and Reach; Flex and Pull

These exercises may be practiced standing, sitting, and/or lying down. Always remember to initiate each exercise with deep

THE MATRIX RELAXATION PROGRAM   137

breathing and follow all the progressive steps as discussed in previous contraction–relaxation exercises. The first exercise in this group, **extend and reach**, is an extension of the wrist and fingers. Open and straighten the fingers. Pull the hand and fingers of each hand back toward the forearm. The tension is felt on the back of the hand and the back of the forearm below the elbow. A little pain might be felt near the wrist. This is ligament stretch; don't overdo it. Synchronize the exercise with breathing, inhaling as you stretch the fingers and exhaling as you relax. Do this several times, making sure to give a proper rest period in between in order to rest and focus on the relaxation. Now add extension of the elbow. Pull the fingers and hand back as before, straighten the elbows and press the arms against the sides. You should feel tension in the back of the forearm, back of the upper arm, and the shoulders. Breathe in, contract, hold it, and exhale while feeling the tension leave the muscles. Rest, relax and concentrate on the relaxation. Repeat five times and rest. (Fig. 12.15.)

The other exercise in this group, **flex and pull**, is flexion of the fingers, wrist, and elbow joints. Bend the fingers into a fist, flex the wrist and move the fist toward the forearm, then flex the elbow and move the forearm toward the upper arm. Feel the tension in the large muscle mass of the forearm flexors and biceps. Synchronize

Fig. 12.15

the tension and relaxation with your breathing. Repeat five times, then rest. (Fig. 12.16.)

Exercise D2. Wall Reach; Sky Reach; Shoulder Roll, Back Reach; Shoulder Elevation

Chances are that you have noticed in yourself or others that after hours of writing or other desk work the natural tendency is to try to stretch out those cramped fingers, elbows, and shoulders. It is a natural reaction, but most people start too late. First of all, they should have prepared themselves better, and second, they should have stopped more frequently and stretched before cramps developed. This is the purpose of this set of exercises. The emphasis is on the relaxation that follows the recoil of the stretch. Sense it, and sense the difference between that feeling and muscle tension.

The first exercise in this group is the **wall reach**, which is done in the standing position. Stand in front of a wall so that your outstretched arms just reach the wall. Place the palms of your hands against the wall. Now step back about 6 inches. Extending your arms primarily from the shoulder, reach for the wall. At the same time spread your fingers and extend them backward. When you make contact with the wall, your shoulder, elbow, wrist, and finger joints should be at full extension and

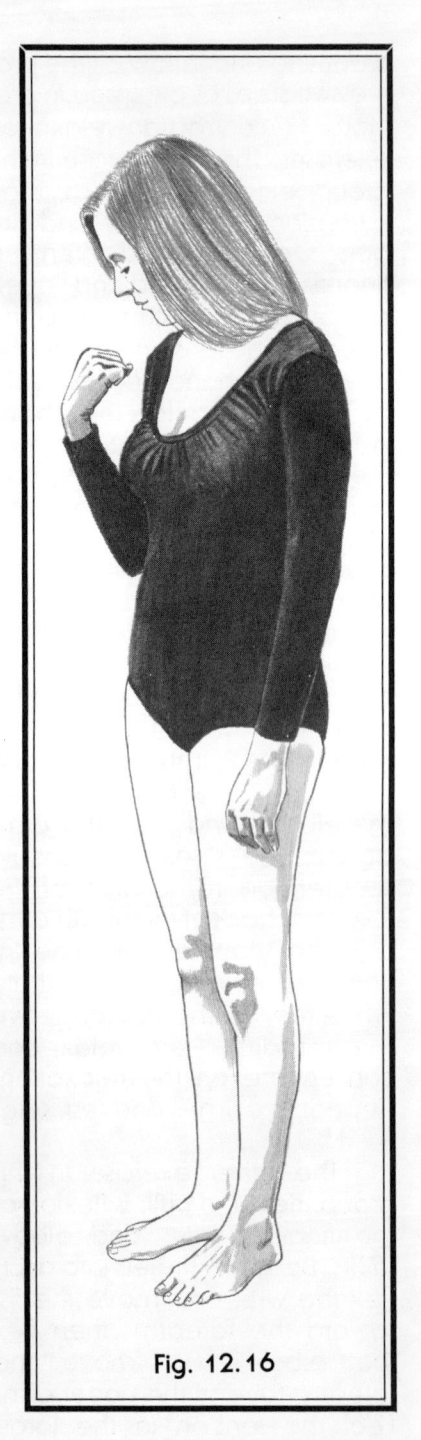

Fig. 12.16

THE MATRIX RELAXATION PROGRAM   139

stretch. Hold the stretch for a count of five and return. Repeat five times. (Fig. 12.17.)

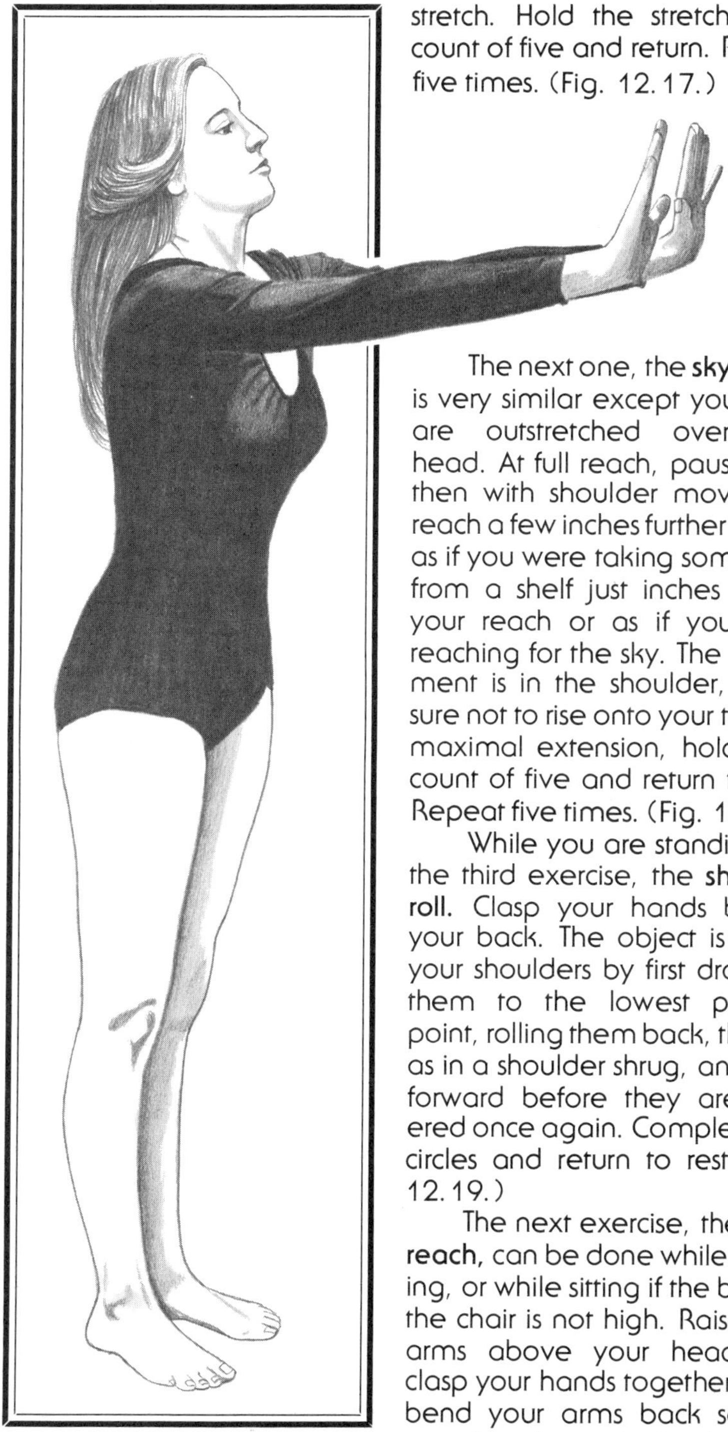

The next one, the **sky reach**, is very similar except your arms are outstretched over your head. At full reach, pause, and then with shoulder movement reach a few inches further almost as if you were taking something from a shelf just inches out of your reach or as if you were reaching for the sky. The movement is in the shoulder, so be sure not to rise onto your toes. At maximal extension, hold for a count of five and return to rest. Repeat five times. (Fig. 12.18.)

While you are standing, do the third exercise, the **shoulder roll**. Clasp your hands behind your back. The object is to roll your shoulders by first dropping them to the lowest possible point, rolling them back, then up as in a shoulder shrug, and then forward before they are lowered once again. Complete five circles and return to rest. (Fig. 12.19.)

The next exercise, the **back reach**, can be done while standing, or while sitting if the back of the chair is not high. Raise your arms above your head and clasp your hands together. Then bend your arms back so that your hands touch the back of

Fig. 12.17

140 THE STRESS MESS SOLUTION

your neck. Pause, and then stretch so that your hands touch a point further down your back. Hold the extreme position for a count of five, then rest. Repeat five times. (Fig. 12.20.)

Fig. 12.18

Fig. 12.19

THE MATRIX RELAXATION PROGRAM 141

The last exercise, **shoulder elevation,** is done either sitting on the floor or standing. Clasp your hands behind your back, allowing them to rest comfortably against your buttocks. Keeping your back straight, raise your arms as high as possible. Hold in the extreme position for a count of five and return to the resting position, but do not unclasp hands. Feel the stretch in shoulders, elbows, and wrists. Feel the relaxation as you return to rest. Repeat five times. (Fig. 12.21.)

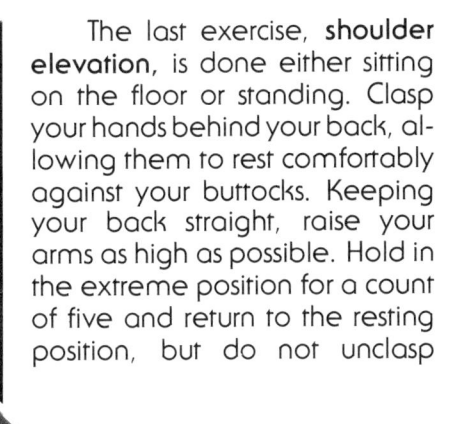

Fig. 12.21

Fig. 12.20

Exercise D3. Arms Heavy and Warm

By now you should be familiar with the procedure for this exercise. It will be quiet concentration of heaviness and warmth in the arms and hands. If you had any success with this exercise in Columns B and C, you will do very well here. If you had difficulty with those previous exercises, this one should provide you with a breakthrough. The reasons are that you have finer control over hands and arms than over legs and trunk, more nerves innervating fewer muscles, and just more practice in using the upper extremities. You may sit or lie down. Start with a few deep breaths. Center yourself. Close your eyes and concentrate on your hands and arms. Your statements are as follows. Repeat them to yourself slowly and quietly:

I am relaxed.
I am calm.
I am quiet.
My right arm is heavy.
My right arm is heavy and warm.
My right arm is warm.
My right arm is warm and relaxed.
I am calm and quite relaxed.
My left arm is heavy.
My left arm is heavy and warm.
My left arm is warm.
My left arm is warm and relaxed.
I am calm and quite relaxed.
My body is warm and relaxed.
I am quiet and at peace.
I am relaxed.

This activity should take about 5 minutes. When you are finished, remain quiet and flow directly into Exercise D4.

Exercise D4. Relaxing Your Grip

If working with another person, just sit back and have him/her read the directions. If you are working by yourself, read the situation, get the idea of what you are being asked to do, then sit back, close your eyes, and work through it. Either way, always close your eyes because it greatly increases your powers of concentration.

Situation 1.

Close your eyes, but in your mind's eye see a tense person. It may be someone you know well or just someone you have seen once. What does this person look like when he/she is stressed?

What is the person doing with his/her legs . . . arms . . . face? Concentrate on the hands and arms. Are they moving or still? Are the hands clenched into a fist or are they open? Are they pushing down onto the arms of the chair? Are they gripping? Are they crossed in front of the body? Are they tensely straight?

Now, assume that position yourself. Place your arms as you see the imagined person doing. Tense your muscles as the person tensed the muscles. See yourself in that position. Feel yourself in that position. Where are you? Who are you with? What message (verbal or nonverbal-implied) is the person giving to you? What is he/she expecting from you? Are you feeling pushed to do something you do not want to do? Or are you feeling held back from doing something you want to do? Now leave those thoughts and rest for a moment.

Situation 2.

Close your eyes and switch your mind's eye to a person whom you see as being very relaxed. How is this person sitting? Concentrate on his/her arms and hands. How are they different from those of the tense person? Assume the relaxed position yourself. Where are you? Who are you with? Do you feel free to do what you want to do? In the absence of expectations this is how your body feels. You can help yourself demand your personal freedom by telling your body to position itself in this fashion. Now slowly open your eyes and reorient yourself to the world around you. Feel the energy flowing through your system vitalizing your sense of commitment to your purpose and to yourself. When you feel someone is pushing you or holding you back, assume this freedom posture and be aware how you are more willing to demand your personal freedom.

Column E: Neck, Head, and Face

Exercise E1. Head Rotation; Teeth Clenching

The primary exercise in this group is **head rotation**. The muscles in this region are overworked as we tend to hold a steady partial tension for hours at a time, especially while doing desk work or driving. **Caution:** individuals with chronic neck problems should use extreme care. The emphasis is on feeling the contraction of the muscles, but the neck is a delicate area; do not strain. Close your eyes. Touch your chin to your breastbone. Return to normal position and rest for a breath, then move the head backward

144 THE STRESS MESS SOLUTION

toward the spine. Return, rest, and then rotate the head so as to look over the right shoulder. Return, rest for a breath, and then look over the left shoulder. Consider these four moves as one exercise and complete them in succession, but do not hurry.

Synchronize each move with your breathing. Inhale as you contract, hold the contraction and your breath for five counts, relax for a few breaths, and continue with the next movement. Repeat the entire sequence five times. (Fig. 12.22.)

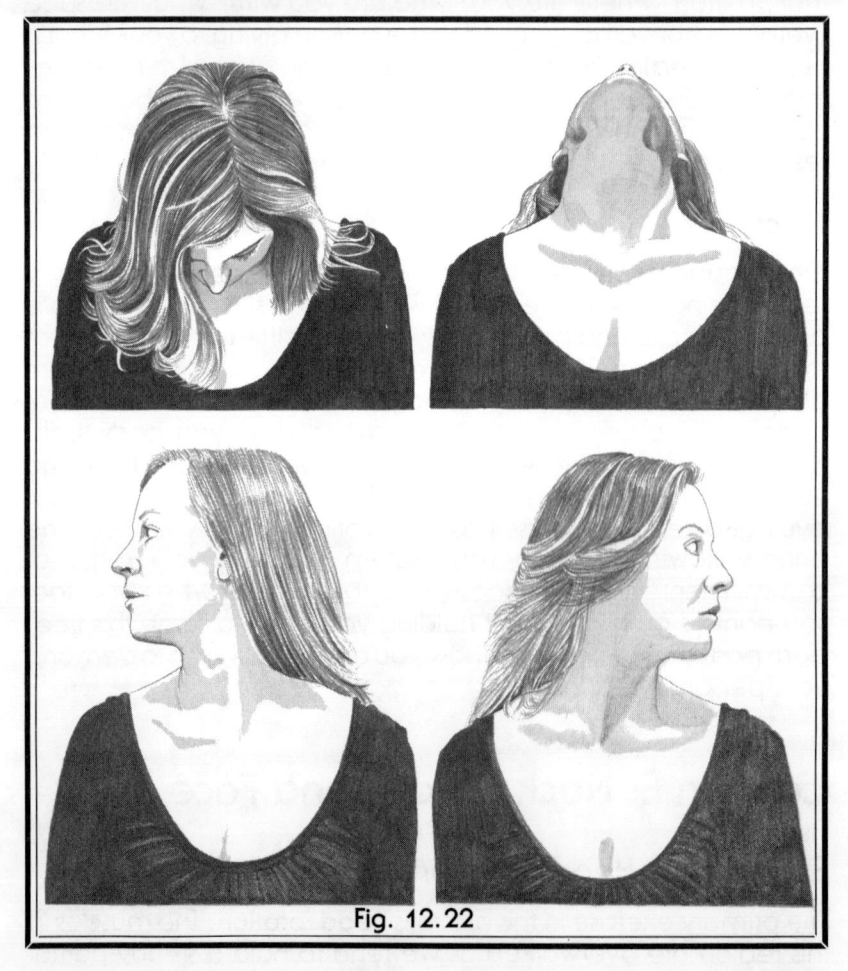

Fig. 12.22

Another group of overworked muscles is the facial muscles, especially the ones involved in talking and chewing. To exercise these, **clench your teeth** together, drawing your face with an expression of surprise over the forehead muscles. Always remember the correct emphasis on breathing! Inhale as you contract and exhale as you relax. Repeat five times and then relax. (Fig. 12.23.)

Fig. 12.23

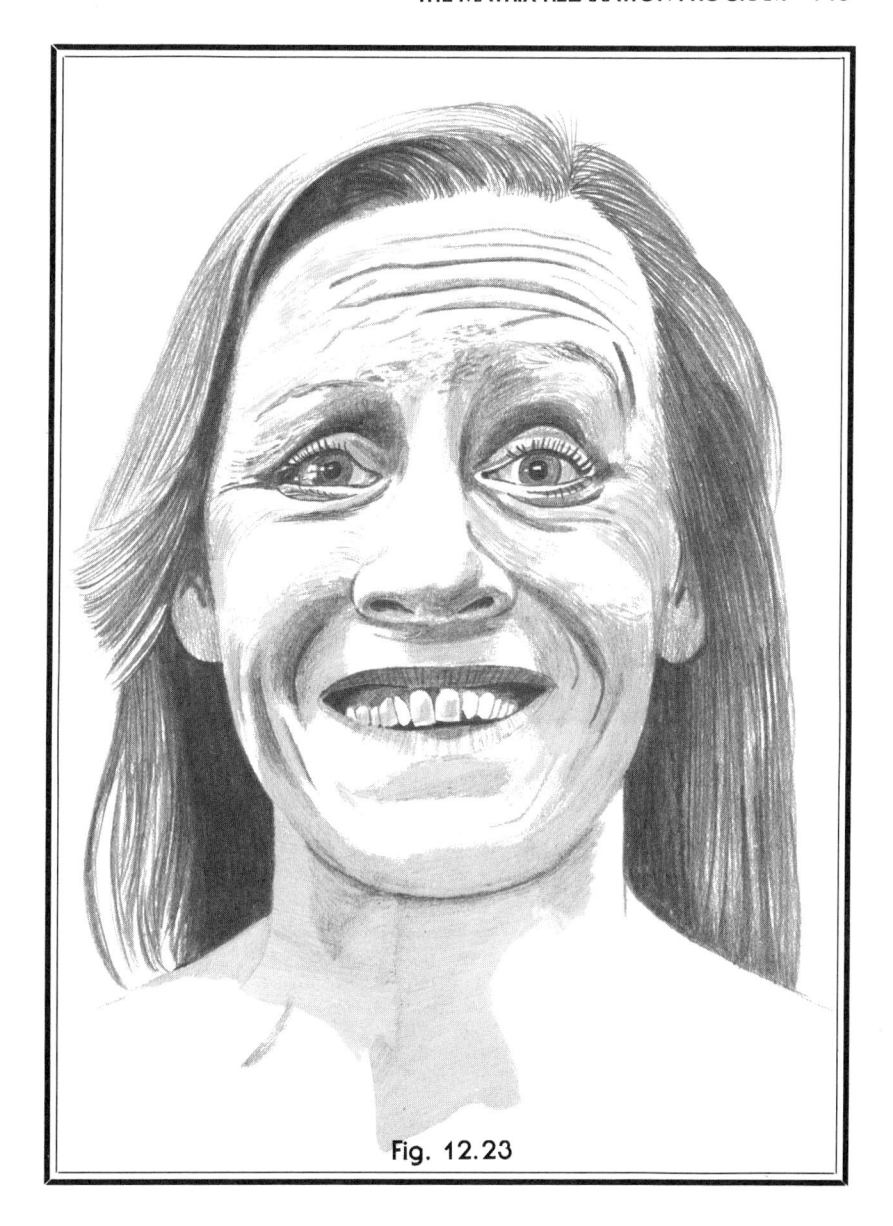

Exercise E2. Neck Stretch; Forced Stretch; Head Roll

If you are going to do any one set of exercises in this book, this set should be the one. Relieving the tension in the neck muscles will do wonders for your total body tension level. We could fill the next ten pages citing the evidence and psychophysiological rationale for the involvement of these muscles in ailments such as tension headaches. These exercises deal directly with the tension of the

146 THE STRESS MESS SOLUTION

neck, shoulders, and upper back, and you will notice instant relief.

Again, we caution if you have a medical problem with your neck, consult your physician before doing the neck exercises. And even if you do not have a problem, be careful not to overdo, as the neck is a delicate area. These exercises may be done while sitting or standing.

The first exercise is the **forward, backward neck stretch,** as shown previously. Move your head slowly back toward your spine until your nose is pointed straight up in the air. Feel the stretch in the front of the neck. Feel the muscles and skin pull tight from the chin. By the way, this will help any saggy double chin problem. Hold for a count of five and slowly move your chin toward your chest. Try to get your chin to your chest, but be sure to keep your back straight—don't cheat. When you get as far forward as you can, try to completely relax the neck muscles. Allow the head to just "dangle loose." Hold for a count of five and return to an upright position by slowly contracting your neck and back muscles. Slowly—no fast jerky movement should be made during any of these exercises. Repeat five times. (Fig. 12.24.)

The second exercise is the **side-to-side neck stretch.** This is not a turn or a roll. It is simply laying the head on the shoulder or as close to it as possible. Start to the right. Slowly just let the head move to your extreme position. Don't force it. Hold for a count of five and return. Pause for a breath in the upright position and let the head move to the left. Hold for a count of five and return. Repeat five times and relax.

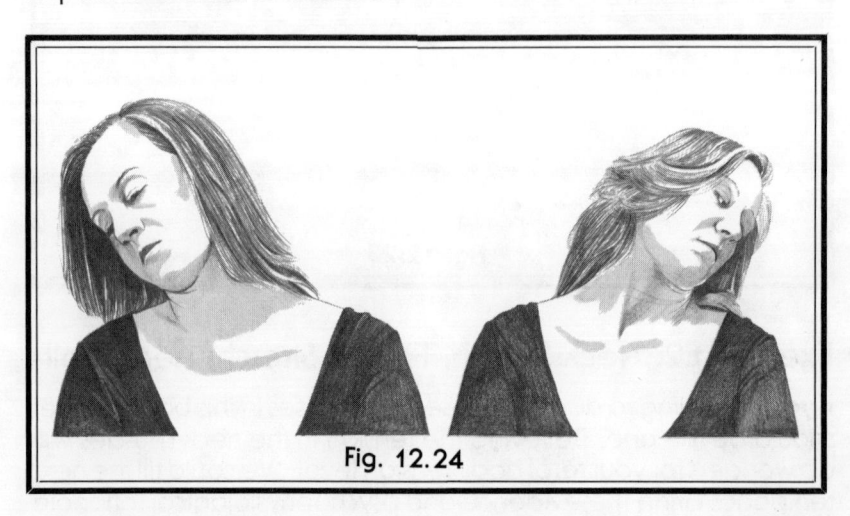

Fig. 12.24

Now that you are limbered up a little, try the **forced stretch.** Lie down on your stomach. Raise your head, keeping your elbows on the floor. Clasp your hands behind your head and slowly and gently push your head toward your chest. Hold for a count of five and return. Next, you will move your head, first to the right, by placing your chin in your right hand, holding the back of your head with the left hand, still keeping your elbows on the floor. Slowly allow your hands to twist your head to the right. Allow your neck muscles to relax and your head to be loose in your hands. Hold in the extreme position for a count of five and return. Change hand positions and turn head to the left. Do all three exercises in order with a slight pause between each one. Repeat the entire sequence five times. (Fig. 12.25.)

Fig. 12.25

The last exercise in this set is the **head roll**. Roll the head to form a complete circle. The idea is to try to keep the head in the extreme stretched position during the entire circle. Try to keep the head in contact with chest, shoulders, and back as you pass them in sequence. The first move is chin to chest and then, starting toward the right, rotate five times. Pause for a breath after each rotation. Then rotate five times starting to the left. Go very slowly. Relax the neck muscles, and allow the head to hang loose. Feel the stretch, feel the sense of tension relief.

Exercise E3. Your Special Place

Recall a time in your life when you felt very relaxed, peaceful, and tranquil. It may help to close your eyes, relax, and let the images come to you.

Describe the place in the following terms:
a. When was it: _____
b. Who were you with: _____
   Note: Even though you might have traveled with another person, do not list that person unless his or her image is vividly associated with the relaxation feeling.
c. Where was it? Look around, describe what you see, describe your feelings and sensations: _____
_____
_____

The place you have described here is your relaxation place. Use it in the following exercise.

Putting It All Together—The 8-Minute Relaxation Plan

Minute 1   In a quiet room and in a comfortable chair assume a restful position and quiet passive attitude. Take four deep breaths. Make each one deeper than the one before. Hold number one for 4 seconds, number two for 5 seconds, number three for 6 seconds, and number four for 7 seconds. Pull the tension from all parts of your body into your lungs and exhale it with each expiration. Feel more relaxed with each breath.

Minute 2   Count backward from ten to zero. Breathe naturally, and with each exhalation count one number and feel more and more relaxed as you approach zero. With each count you descend a relaxation stairway and become more deeply relaxed until you are totally relaxed at zero.

Minute 3-7   Now go to that relaxation place outlined earlier in the exercise. Stay there for 4 minutes. Try to recall vividly, but passively, the feelings of that place and time that were very relaxing.

Minute 8 Bring your attention back to yourself. Count from one to ten. Energize your body. Feel the energy, vitality, and health flow through your system. Feel alert, and eager to resume your activities. Open your eyes.

Exercise E4. Removing Your Mask

If working with another person, just sit back and have him/her read the directions. If you are working by yourself, read the situation, get the idea of what you are being asked to do, then sit back, close your eyes, and work through it. Either way, always close your eyes because it greatly increases your powers of concentration.

Situation 1.

Close your eyes, but in your mind's eye see a tense person. It may be someone you know well or just someone you have seen once. What does this person look like when he/she is stressed? What is the person doing with his/her legs . . . arms . . . face? Concentrate on the head, neck, and face. Are the eyes wide open or squinted? Is the head pulled down and the shoulders up? Is the forehead wrinkled? Are the jaws tightly clenched? Are the neck muscles tightly drawn?

Now, assume that position yourself. Place your head, neck, and face as you see the imagined person doing. Tense your muscles as the person tensed the muscles. See yourself in that position. Feel yourself in that position. Where are you? Who are you with? What message (verbal or nonverbal-implied) is the person giving to you? What is he/she expecting from you? Are you feeling pushed to do something you do not want to do? Or are you feeling held back from doing something you want to do? Now leave those thoughts and rest for a minute.

Situation 2.

Close your eyes and switch your mind's eye to a person whom you see as being very relaxed. How is this person sitting? Concentrate on the head, neck, and face. How are they different from those of the tense person? Assume that relaxed position yourself. Where are you? Who are you with? Do you feel free to do what you want to do? In the absence of expectations this is how your body feels. You can help yourself demand your personal freedom by telling your body to position itself in this fashion. Now, slowly open your eyes and reorient yourself to the world around you. Feel the energy flowing through your system vitalizing your sense of commitment to your purpose and to yourself. When you feel someone is pushing you or holding you back, assume this freedom posture and be aware of how you are more willing to demand your personal freedom.

Chapter 13

Stress Reduction and Relaxation Through Physical Activity

Except for minor differences in cosmetics, there is virtually no difference between the modern individual and medieval individual or for that matter the cave dweller. Our limbs are the same, our organs are the same, our physiological processes including our stress responses are the same. To a large degree it was the stress response which ensured our survival by supplying what was needed to "rise to the occasion": the increased alertness for the hunt, the increased strength and anger for the fight, the increased energy and endurance to run when fighting seemed unwise. The stressed state was, and is, a distinctly different psychophysiological state tucked away in ready reserve for that moment when survival hangs in the balance. Mother Nature also endowed us with a built-in drive to conserve our energies for that time when our lives need the stress response; thus quite naturally we developed an innate drive to become personally energy efficient. Understandably, we became supermotivated to develop tools and eventually machines to help conserve this lifesaving energy, and to band together in groups for protection.

As they say, "the rest is history." What ensued appears as the ultimate success story. The development of technology and society has made the stress response less necessary and somewhat obsolete. Chances are that over the next million or so years the stress response will gradually evolve out of existence. However, in the meantime we are more or less caught between a rock and a hard place. We have this highly efficient stress response system which periodically excites our entire physical system to save our lives, but the saber-toothed tiger turns out to be our boss criticizing our work, knowledge that our mother-in-law is coming to visit for a month, or the fact that someone is driving too slow in the fast lane in front of us.

In Chapter I of this book we defined stress as a physical response to a psychosocial situation and outlined the categories of stress reduction that an individual could implement as generally being 1) reducing the incidence of stress-inducing situations, 2) using relaxation to recondition our stress responsiveness, 3) physically utilizing the physical stress products. The primary contribution of physical activity is the dissipation or using up of the stress products which are produced by fear, threats to our ego, or whatever has evoked the hormonal and nervous systems into defensive postures. A second benefit of physical activity is that it decreases our reactivity to future stress by conditioning relaxation. A third contribution is engendered in the postexercise feeling of well-being, tranquility, and transcendence.

Physical Activity After Stress Arousal

Following the three benefits of physical activity outlined above, let's first look at physical activity used after stress arousal as a means to restore relaxation. See yourself in a work situation being asked to give more time that you want to give, to do more work than you want to do. This situation puts strain on your personal relations at home. You are being pushed and pulled until an underlying state of tension becomes part of your life. Then the straw that breaks the camel's back is dropped as your boss berates you in front of your coworkers and you experience a massive stress response. Anger, fear, indignation, rage boil through your body. This is the response described many times before: the hormonal and nervous systems ready the body for fight or flight and now is the time for action, physical action.

It is important to recognize that this stress response was developed to end in physical activity. The increased heart and respiration rates are to pump blood and oxygen to active muscles and stimulated control centers of the brain. The outpouring of sugars and fats into the blood are meant to feed the muscles. This is no time to sit and feel all of these sensations tearing away at the body; this is the time to **move**, to use up these stress products, to exonerate the body of the destructive forces that stress can exert on those who remain sedentary. Appropriate activity in this case would be total body exercise such as swimming, running, dancing, biking, or active, dual, or team sports that last about an hour. (This is assuming adequate physical conditioning to perform the task.) It is also good to remember that stress arousal in such a situation will alter many physical systems for more than 24 hours with no additional stressors applied. The exercise will be most beneficial if done within a few hours of the stress arousal, but any time during the following 24 hours will help. Also important is the fact that such a situation almost always serves to upset the daily routine enough to make almost everything that follows more stressful than it would normally be without the stress episode.

The picture that should be coming clear by now is that the

stress response is a preparation for physical activity. Thus, a natural release is bodily movement. It is a treatment form that everyone can afford. And if you are not into running, swimming, or playing games, don't forget good old-fashioned physical work, be it productive or somewhat contrived. For example, a friend of ours who happens to be a basketball coach realized that he became very uptight during games and therefore did the following activity after each game. He had a pile of dirt in his back yard which he would move from point A to point B and back again as many times as needed until he felt his stress level subside. To some extent we are all coaches of a sort: we watch the game being played, we get emotionally involved, and then we sit back and suffer the consequences of not interacting physically. The key factor for each of us is to recognize when we are stressed and act physically on that response soon after.

Physical Activity Before Stress Arousal

Another important aspect of physical activity is that it can be preventive in nature. The values in this regard are so potent that if they could be bottled and sold for people to take a dose a day, the bottling and sales agents would be rich beyond compare, so effective is the product.

During physical activity all the body systems are stimulated for action. After the activity, the systems rebound by slowing down, thus promoting relaxation and tranquility. About 90 minutes after a good bout of exercise there occurs a feeling of deep relaxation. If you are a chronic exerciser, you know that feeling and perhaps are aware of its lasting effects throughout the day. The relaxation that comes after exercise brings with it a certain imperturbability, a lowered reactivity to the environment that helps the chronic exerciser to react more appropriately to stimuli. It makes your step a little lighter, your attitude more positive, and it takes more to get you upset.

In addition to achieving the feeling of tranquility, you use up stress products daily rather than waiting for psychosocial stressors to trigger them. This technique calls for a regular exercise program, but you must be extremely future-oriented to exercise today for benefits that will accrue tomorrow. In a nutshell that is why most people fail to maintain a regular exercise program. They know they are doing it for preventive reasons, for how much better they will feel tomorrow, for how much longer they will live. Most of us are now centered. We do things now and we want the benefits now. So if you choose an activity that is not enjoyable, just because it is good for you tomorrow, chances are that you will not practice it very long. Exercising with a partner, joining a club, or making certain to engage in activities enjoyable to you is helpful and relates to the third reason for exercise—general well-being.

Physical Activity for Well-Being and Transcendence

Most regular exercisers feel better about themselves when they exercise. It just feels right when they do it and wrong when they do not. It enhances positive feelings toward themselves which bounce off others a positive energy; it helps make life complete. The tranquility state, the oneness, the internal calm that have been experienced by those who really get involved in their activity make their exercise programs a necessity; these people are almost addicted to the feeling it gives them. There is little mystery as to why this happens; exercise is perhaps our most natural form of expression. We were made to move and, when we do, we rediscover the original unifying thread of the mind and body. My wife recently took up regular exercise in the form of running, and as she is a very present-centered person I asked her why she runs. Her response was: "I have been getting up every single morning and running 3½ miles and right now I am loving my body running. I love my hair flopping on my neck, massaging my head, seeming to stimulate my hair follicles. I like hearing my breath meeting the wind. I like feeling my lungs expand as they take in more air. I like the feeling of my leg muscles becoming taut and supporting me, bouncing me, throwing me into the air, and then relaxing for a moment, then becoming taut again. I am liking my shoulders feeling loose and dropping around my neck, kind of flopping as I run, feeling relaxed in a part of all of me. I like the nowness of my running, I like the nowness of my health. I continue to do it because I like the way it makes me feel now, and how it is going to make me feel tomorrow, and I am constantly finding more creative ways to like it now."

You will notice that even though she talked about herself, she talked about feeling and not about her ego. She was not competing with me or any of her woman friends. She was not ego-involved. This is an important point, for to get all of the benefits of the exercise one must choose an activity that is **not ego-involved**. Playing a highly competitive game of golf and wrapping a putter around a tree is not a relaxing activity. Nor is a game of tennis when your ego rests on each shot.

We are competitive people with a competitive heritage. We compete for money, jobs, space, and glorification of the ego. It may seem odd that our leisure and recreation activities, intended as diversions from competition, are likewise competitive, but we have become conditioned to seek ego enhancement from beating others, and just because we are not on the job, there is no reason to believe that we can stop competing. Most of us are competition addicts and we measure ourselves by comparison to others. It was previously mentioned that exercise will "burn off" much of the stress arousal products, but competitive exercise often creates **more** stress in the form of lingering self-doubt, anger, and embarrassment. Think about your recreational activities. How transcendental are they? Do you lose your sense of time; do the hours seem like minutes? Or do you lose your temper and/or patience with yourself and others? Do you lose your sense of self? Or are you constantly watching yourself and admonishing yourself for bad performance?

Competitive sports are not the only leisure activities which are the culprits here. Performance of singular activities (such as running or skiing) is no guarantee of ego transcendence. "Can I run 3 miles? Am I running as fast today as yesterday? What if I can't make it the entire distance? I really don't have it any more. Why can't I make a simple parallel turn? Mary can do it, why can't I? I don't think I am skiing any better this year than last year." Some activities are not directly competitive, in that there is no winner and no loser in each event, but we can make them just as competitive as if we win or lose by constantly rating our performance against our past performances or against the performance of others (we even take it upon ourselves to compare our performance with that of a professional athlete!). What is more important, we allow the performance to influence our feelings about ourselves. "It seems as though any reasonably intelligent and halfway coordinated person should be able to learn to ski in a year, so why can't I? What kind of a person can't even run one mile without stopping?" This is the "terrible athlete, therefore terrible person" syndrome.

In two important books on play, Tim Gallwey (1976, 1977) touched the essence of the ego-void state called **Self II**, which is the noncritical, inherent athlete in all of us who can perform without constant self-instruction. It is the part of us that hits that "lucky shot" and is responsible for the better performance which often paradoxically accompanies not really trying. Unfortunately, most of us have enslaved our Self II by our critical, ego-protecting, self-directing Self I. Again, we might look at this attitude as a conditioned response in our society. We have spent so many years being educated by learning and analyzing with our minds that we have lost faith and ability to let Self II take over, to get lost in the joy of movement, to flow with the feeling of the activity, and to correct movements through somatic and visual feedback, not through highly critical mental examination in which we paralyze ourselves by overanalysis.

One does not have to be a stock market analyst to realize that one of the fastest growing industries in the world is recreation. True, we have more leisure time and we need to fill a void, but beyond that, people are beginning to recognize that it is very difficult to remain healthy performing only sedentary tasks. So while some are driven to play via physical activity to counter boredom, others are trying to prevent degenerative diseases, and still others are driven to activity because the activity itself is "right" and reinforcing. To many, physical activity is the only transcending experience they have ever had, so they seek to reproduce the feeling and search for more active leisure pursuits.

Unfortunately, the modern man and woman (at least in the industrialized world) are obsessed with recreation and pursue it with the same diligence and competition with which they pursue work. In fact, for many the only difference between work and recreation is that one may be done behind a desk and the other is done on a golf course. Everything else is the same. Critical analysis is present, as are competition and ego defense, so the participant is often left with self-doubt and extended worry over performance and its reflection on personality and character. In order for you to use a physical activity as a relaxation technique, it must be void of competition and ego involvement; otherwise it is a mere diversion of your time.

The Activity Self-Assessment table for measuring your activity level lists activities which are daily routine for many people. In addition, a sample of other activities is given. If you engage in an activity other than those listed, try to approximate that activity with one given here and use the points accorded to it. Having completed the exercise, you will have 24 hours of activity listed. For each hour or partial hour, multiply the weighted score given for the activity and then total the points. This is your physical activity score.

In addition to filling our the Activity Self-Assessment, answer the four questions dealing with your motivational state and physical activity.

If you score below 40 points, you are a very sedentary person and should consider engaging in an activity which is higher in the point system than the activities you usually engage in. If you score above 55, you are probably enjoying the benefits of physical

ACTIVITY SELF-ASSESSMENT

HOW MANY HOURS PER DAY DO YOU SPEND:

Sleeping	____hours	@ .85 points/hr	____
Sitting		@ 1.5 points/hr	
riding/driving	____hours		
study/desk work	____hours		
meals	____hours		
watching TV	____hours		
reading	____hours		
other	____hours		
	____hours		
	____hours	(total sitting × 1.5)	____
Standing		@ 2 points/hr	
standing	____hours		
dressing	____hours		
showering	____hours		
other	____hours		
	____hours	(total standing × 2)	____
Walking			
slow walk	____hours	@ 3 points/hr	____
moderate speed	____hours	@ 4 points/hr	____
very fast walk	____hours	@ 5 points/hr	____
Occupational housework, light physical work	____hours	@ 3 points/hr	____
Heavy total body physical exertion			
rapid calisthenics	____hours	@ 4 points/hr	____
slow run (jog)	____hours	@ 6 points/hr	____
fast run	____hours	@ 7 points/hr	____
recreational racket sports	____hours	@ 8 points/hr	____
competitive racket sports	____hours	@ 9–10 points/hr	____
Stair climbing	____hours	@ 8 points/hr	____
	24 hours	TOTAL POINTS	

Do you have an exercise outlet for stress buildup?   Yes__No__
Do you use it?   Yes__No__
Do you exercise regularly for its preventive rewards?   Yes__No__
Have you discovered the transcendental
  nature of exercise?   Yes__No__

activity. If you are physically able, you should have some regular activity which is worth more than 5 points per hour. To be a "chronic exerciser" you should perform that 5+ point activity five times a week for at least one half hour per bout.

Concerning the last questions on the exercise, if you do not use physical activity to burn off stress products, try it. Choose an activity compatible to you and your lifestyle; some good ones are listed on the following pages. Do it long enough for it to be physically effective—you will need to walk longer than you run to use up similar energy or stress products. If you find you can tolerate this activity, try doing it regularly so you can keep a low stress profile. And if you really learn to love the activity, you will recognize the rewards and want to share them with others.

Walking.

This is one of the universally popular activities. While the energy use is only moderate, walking can be done for long periods of time and seems to be very soothing and relaxing. There is no cost for equipment, and special facilities are not required. Everyone can participate in it and it can be done year around. Walking does take a lot of time and one must walk quite fast if it is going to be used for a conditioning exercise. One especially good feature about it is that you can walk and talk at the same time, and as it relaxes, it seems to promote relaxed, positive conversation.

Jogging.

Running 5 miles per hour or less is considered jogging. It utilizes a moderate amount of energy and is thus a very good stress reducer for those of moderate physical conditioning. Further, it promotes weight loss, builds cardiovascular endurance, and strengthens the legs. Like walking, it requires no special facilities and, except for proper shoes, it costs no money. Jogging may be hard on knees and ankle joints and new participants should have a physical examination.

Running.

Maintaining a pace faster than 5 miles per hour is running. Energy output is about maximum; thus it requires a relatively shorter time to deliver results. It promotes weight loss, cardiovascular conditioning, and well-being to the point where it is the fastest growing sport in the world. Good shoes, good physical conditioning, and a physical examination before beginning are a must. Running can be hard on joints.

Swimming.

Swimming can be very beneficial. It possesses all of the benefits of running without the drawbacks of being potentially jarring to the joints. The problem is that few people who go to a swimming pool actually swim. Swimming for exercise is swimming laps, keeping moving. If you are an exercise swimmer you will know the tremendous effort required. Of course, you must have a pool to swim in and you must be somewhat skillful.

Dancing.

Dancing is like swimming in that results depend on how hard you work at it. Aerobic dancing and fast disco dancing can be excellent for stress reduction, body conditioning, and feelings of well-being. It requires a knowledge of the steps, some coordination, or a lot of guts. It can be done year around.

Biking.

This activity calls for good energy output, promotes conditioning, and is easier on joints than running or jogging. The bike does cost money and requires some skill. Biking can be a social activity and of course it can be energy-saving transportation.

Alpine skiing.

This type of skiing utilizes energy in varying amounts depending on how long and sustained the effort is. It promotes conditioning, especially in the legs. It is social and enjoyable and usually promotes feelings of well-being. Skiing does require a learned skill and expensive equipment. It is one of those sports in which the talk often centers around constantly trying to analyze and improve skill. This often leads to tension and negative feelings if you get yourself into the vicious cycle of "I am a bad skier, therefore a bad person." Ski racing often tends to become too competitive.

Cross-country skiing.

Excellent for energy output and excellent for stress reduction, cross-country takes you out in nature. It generally is relaxing while being excellent for conditioning. It requires skill and special equipment and of course is seasonal.

Racket sports.

These sports are excellent for energy utilization, stress reduction, and body conditioning if a fast game is played. They require special skills, equipment, and expensive facilities, although most communities have free outdoor tennis courts. The biggest drawback is that these games by their very nature promote competition, invite critical self-analysis, and quite often promote more tension than they relieve. Extreme care must be taken to avoid the overcritical attitude and overcompetitiveness engendered by these games. If handled wisely, they can be enjoyable social activities which, because they demand total concentration, can serve to take your mind off your troubles.

Golf.

Golf can be enjoyable and relaxing if you are not too critical or competitive. It is little value for energy use unless you walk and carry your own clubs. Golf requires skill, expensive equipment, and expensive facilities.

Bowling.

This activity is relaxing and enjoyable if you are not too self-critical and competitive. It is little better than just sitting as far as energy utilization and stress reduction are concerned. Bowling requires some skill and special equipment and moderately priced facilities which are usually available in most communities.

Calisthenics including yoga.

These total body activities have toning and conditioning value, and little skill or equipment is involved. These activities may exacerbate existing muscle or joint problems, though. They tend to promote feelings of well-being in the sense of knowing you are doing something for yourself and your health.

Weight lifting.

A specialized form of calisthenics which promotes body conditioning and energy utilization, weight lifting increases strength, improves the physique, and may improve self-image. It requires special equipment and does have the potential for injury if not done properly, although the skills required are minimal. A physical checkup is necessary for beginners, especially those past the age of 30.

Chapter 14

The Organizational Stress Audit

Up to this point, our Holistic System has consisted of a comprehensive system of strategies designed for the **individual** employee. Such strategies will be effective in any type of organization because they are individually oriented. The fourth and final aspect of our Holistic System for business and industry allows us to focus upon any specific organizational environment as the patient. This organization-oriented perspective gives us the unique opportunity to reduce occupational stress in the most efficient ways possible—by modifying the forces of stress inherent in the organization itself and by providing organizationally sanctioned programs to reduce stress. We call this process the **Organizational Stress Audit** (OSA).

Just as individuals have aspects of their lives which create stress (called **stressors**), an organization can be thought of as having stressor points inherent in its structure or function, and these create stress, as well. The OSA is a process by which the organization is analyzed as to identify stressor points. Strategies are then designed to alleviate their negative impact. The OSA consists of three stages:

Stage I: Organizational stressor diagnosis
Stage II: Design and implementation of in-house stress management installations
Stage III: Monitoring and follow-up procedures

The complete OSA is quite detailed and beyond the scope of the personal orientation of this book. However, once you get into personal stress it is natural (if there are organizational resources available) to examine the organization as a contributing factor to excessive stress. Stress reduction on this level will further help to ease the stress of those who must function within the organization. Below is a skeletal structure for implementing the OSA.

Stage I of the OSA involves diagnosing or identifying aspects of the total work environment which are responsible for creating excessive employee stress. This diagnostic process involves an examination of:

1. The organizational structure
2. The formal organizational communication network.
3. The informal interpersonal communication network

4. The reward systems, intrinsic and extrinsic
5. The nature of the actual work function being performed
6. The psychoenvironmental aspects of the work place
7. The psychological and physiological tolerances of key personnel to high-pressure situations and chronic stress.

To gather information on these aspects of the organization we use four basic data-gathering methodologies. Paper-and-pencil **attitude surveys** are created for each specific organization in order to reach a relatively large number of respondents with questions tailored to the idiosyncracies of each organizational environment. In addition to the attitude survey we place significant effort into **personal interviews** with various individuals. We have found that these interviews have two important functions: 1) they serve as a reality check on the validity of the paper-and-pencil responses, and 2) they serve as a useful tool to uncover additional in-depth information. In effect, an interview is a far more sensitive data-gathering technique. On-site **process observation** offers another method of obtaining information about the stressfulness of any organization. The decision whether to choose external or participant observation will depend upon which method will yield the most information without contaminating or otherwise invalidating that information by the observation process itself. The final data-gathering methodology employed in the OSA is the **stress analysis**. The stress analysis consists of a psychological and medical examination for key personnel, for the purpose of determining a given individual's current level of stress as well as his or her tolerance level for stress. The examination consists of two parts: 1) the administration of a specially designed battery of valid and reliable psychological tests, and 2) the administration of cardiovascular, pulmonary, and hemodynamic examinations. These analyses yield a picture of an individual's current level of stress and his/her mental and physiological stability to withstand acute high-pressure situations and/or chronically elevated stress levels. The stress analysis may serve as a primary prevention methodology for long-time employees or may even be used in hiring and promotion processes when the prospective job involves significant levels of unavoidable stress. There has even been some research conducted on predicting an individual's "weak organ," that is, the organ in the body that is most likely to suffer the ill effects of chronic stress (Everly, 1978a, 1978b). When perfected, this psychophysiological stress profile may allow medical professionals to diagnose a person's weak organ system and then strengthen that organ system in a primary prevention sense, thereby averting the development of many psychosomatic diseases.

Stage II of the OSA consists of analyzing the results of Stage I and designing and implementing modifications in the organization itself to reduce stress levels. Numerous in-house intervention strategies are possible.

One such strategy involves altering the organizational structure to eliminate points of dysfunction. The opinion that most organizations are structured for irrational historical, "political," and interpersonal reasons rather than task-related reasons seems to be true in many cases. Minor structural changes can go a long way in reducing stress.

Altering job function has been found to be an effective remedy for organizational environments that are inherently frustrating, boring, or unrewarding. The techniques of **job enlargement** and **job enrichment** may be used to expand the employee's job functions and provide greater intrinsic rewards. **Job rotation** can be employed to provide workers with different work experiences as they rotate or exchange work roles periodically.

Techniques such as **unitization** and **team building** create conditions in which the workers are given an opportunity to complete entire projects and see the end results of their labors. All of these alterations in job function have been found to be effective in combating frustration due to job roles, overspecialization, fractionalization, and boring work environments.

Recently, a somewhat less traditional stress reduction technique, training in **meditation,** has gained some popularity within industrial settings. Although it originated in the Far East, there have been numerous Western adaptations such as Transcendental Meditation and the Relaxation Response. Companies such as Transco and Faultless Starch/Bon Ami Company have instituted administratively sanctioned meditation programs for their employees. Even the conservative banking industry has used meditation. The Upper Avenue National Bank in Chicago has successfully used it as an in-house training program. The results of meditation have been so favorable in industry that the American Management Association has published a text reviewing its usefulness in business and industry.

A new trend in organizational development interventions is based upon **environmental psychology.** Under this heading considerations about environmental design/architecture, color, sound, lighting, and temperature are made. Psychoenvironmental manipulations may include repainting or refurnishing offices, waiting rooms, and even factories to make them more conducive to the performance of the work done within them. Certain floor designs, interior decorations, and colors have been found to promote productivity while others have been shown to contribute to ineffectiveness and elevated stress levels. Similar research has revealed that certain types of music can facilitate work, increase relaxation, and actually improve motor (involving skeletal muscles) coordination and performance. However, still other forms of music can cause elevated stress levels by being distracting, too loud, or out of synchrony with one's natural bodily rhythms. As we discussed earlier, lighting and temperature can cause stress, yet certain levels of each can facilitate relaxation as well.

Some corporations have taken a **total environment** approach to environmental psychology. Some firms have created relaxation rooms which can be used for relaxation breaks instead of coffee breaks. Other rooms can be designed to facilitate creativity and problem-solving for executives and research and development personnel. Some companies have gone so far as to create business "retreats" for employees. These retreats act as ideal environments for rest, relaxation, and creativity where employees can hold conferences and do other work under optimal conditions. The Japanese industrial complex has developed many of these concepts into realistic operational installations.

A somewhat futuristic in-house installation option which is available and has gained some popularity is the **biofeedback** facility such as that pioneered by the Equitable Life Assurance Society. Biofeedback has the advantage of being highly flexible in its applications. It can be used for general relaxation, for relaxation of specific body parts such as a tense neck, lower back, or shoulders, and for many clinically related problems such as various forms of headaches and even some forms of high blood pressure. Biofeedback has even shown promise as a useful method for increasing problem-solving and creativity skills. It has the disadvantage of requiring specialized and highly sophisticated equipment in many instances. More important, the utilization of biofeedback methods requires a trained biofeedback clinician. Unfortunately biofeedback has been sometimes misused in the past. It has attracted many curious health care practitioners who, while possessing medical or psychological degrees, lack specialized training in biofeedback. This lack of specialized training often results in improper clinical utilization of the biofeedback methodologies which translates to wasted time and money. In general, however, biofeedback facilities can be very worthwhile investments for some companies.

In-house **counseling facilities** represent installations that can be used to effectively combat stress from frustration, change, and stressful personalities. Industrial counseling has been used extensively and with great success by Kennecott Copper Corporation. Counseling can be applied in four different forms: crisis counseling, long-term counseling, career counseling, and psychological assessment and counseling as part of a yearly medical checkup.

Crisis counseling involves having a phone-in and walk-in counseling office which is easily accessible to employees. The purpose is to act as a temporary aid during interpersonal and psychological emergencies for employees.

Longer-term counseling and psychiatric services are another option. Such services would entail facilities for family and marriage counseling as well as individual counseling.

Career counseling is perceived as a major requirement for job satisfaction by many of today's workers. Such counseling facilitates career development decision-making, acts to cushion career changes and crises, and is of particular usefulness in preparing individuals for retirement.

Finally, the psychological assessment and counseling session can be a useful part of an annual medical exam. Such assessment can be used by the medical officer as a preventive medical strategy capable of identifying psychological problems and low stress tolerances before any harm is done. The establishment of a yearly "stress analysis" as described earlier would probably save industry millions of dollars each year in medical costs and lost productivity. The counseling programs at Kennecott return three to six dollars for every one dollar invested. With these kinds of returns the industrial counseling system will soon become a common addition to the large corporate environment.

Some organizations approach stress management through **human relations seminars.** Specific seminars on stress reduction, communication skills, time management, management-by-objectives, and leadership can all be beneficial. In many cases they can increase motivation in addition to disseminating valuable skills in stress management.

Finally, **physical exercise programs** have received a new breath of life in recent years, especially jogging. Corporations have recognized the benefits of installing in-house exercise programs as ways of increasing the mental and physical health of their employees.

The key to successfully implementing Stage II is to tailor the strategies to the needs, personnel, and budget of each individual organization. An improper match will waste time and money.

Stage III consists of establishing a system by which stress levels can be continually monitored. Periodic stress surveys and interviews provide an "early warning" capability in the stress management system. These can be done simply and inexpensively by someone in the personnel or medical department. The merits of this stage are essentially the same as in any prevention-oriented strategy: it costs far less to intervene early, when the problem is small, than it does to wait until the problem is a massive one.

Summary

In summary, the OSA represents an effective **complement** to any individual stress reduction program. The OSA brings to any personal employee-centered stress program the added advantage of being "tailored" for each organization's specific needs, as well as ensuring long-term return on investment (a consideration often overlooked in the implementation of stress management programs).

In application, the OSA represents an attempt to modify the inherent sources of occupational stress and to offer organizationally sanctioned programs to reduce stress as much as is feasible. OSA is to the organization what Human Engineering is to the individual employee.

Conceptually, this is the most efficient process by which to intervene pragmatically; however, this OSA process must be considered as only one component of an overall stress reduction system for business and industry; it is highly contingent upon sufficient resources to complete such an undertaking. In our opinion it remains a complement to the major thrust of an individual employee-centered system as described through most of this book.

EPILOGUE

Congratulations! You now possess enough information to make your job and your life less stressful. But before you close the book, let us have one last chance to put this experience into perspective. Let's examine what it is that you now know that you did not know before, what skills you now have that you did not have before, how you see yourself and your world differently now than you did before.

You may not be an accountant, and you may never have been in the exact situation as was Jack, but all of us experience the same sort of stress and all of us make that stress worse through similar internal dialogue. The realities of stress are that: 1) stress can cause physical dysfunction and illness, and in addition to the human suffering there are billions of dollars lost to society each year, 2) we all experience some degree of stress daily, and many of us, like the frog discussed in Chapter 1, do not realize how hot our water is, and 3) stress is part stressful environment and partly the stories we tell ourselves about our environment, or in other words, how we react to our stressful world. In Part II of this book you constructed your own personal stress profile, so now you know what makes your world stressful.

A closer look into the world of work-related stress reveals that no job is so inherently stressful that much of the stress cannot be exorcized, and no individual is so out of control that he or she cannot reduce personal stress. This brings us to the ultimate reality: you, your abilities, and your motivations. Ability comes in two forms, what you know and what you can do. Knowledge of the techniques is essential, but unless you put them into practice, adopt them as components of your lifestyle, they are just interesting bits of information taking up brain storage space along with remembering the distance from Jupiter to Mars or your mother-in-law's telephone number.

Stress is made up of multiple factors. Thus we have presented a multifaceted stress reduction program—the Holistic Approach to stress management—consisting of four strategies, three of them personal-centered and one organizational-centered. As successful as these strategies have been, our years of research and clinical practice have taught us that they are only as good as one's motivation to use them. We have found that people do not practice what they know because they do not believe they have the power to guide their own destinies. If you argue long enough and loudly enough for your limitations, then eventually they will become yours. But the reverse is also true. If you proclaim your power, it too will be yours. The ultimate decision is **yours**. The strategies work. Only you can decide to use them and ultimately allow them to work for you.

References

Adcock, R. L. The Time Management Process. Unpublished Master's Thesis, Florida State Univ., 1970.

Bass, B. M., and G. V. Barrett. Man, Work, and Organization. Boston: Allyn and Bacon, 1972.

Bennis, W. G. Changing Organizations. New York: McGraw-Hill, 1966.

Benson, H. The Relaxation Response. New York: Morrow, 1975.

Colligan, M. J., and W. Stockton. The mystery of assembly line hysteria. Psychology Today, June 1978, 93-114.

Cooper, C. L., and R. Payne. Stress at Work. New York: Wiley, 1978.

Dembroski, J. M., et al. Physiologic reactions to social challenge in persons evidencing the Type A coronary-prone behavior pattern. Journal of Human Stress, 3, (1977), 2–9.

Drucker, P. F. The Practice of Management. New York: Harper, 1954.

Everly, G. S. The Organ Specificity Score as a Measure of Psychophysiological Stress Reactivity. Doctoral dissertation, University of Maryland, College Park, 1978a.

———. Selected psychometric properties of the Organ Specificity Score as a component of a stress profile. In AAHPER, Research Consortium, Volume I, Book 2. Washington, D.C.: AAHPER, 1978b.

———. Psychophysiological and biofeedback methodologies for the assessment of community "stress education" programs. Paper presented at the Lifelong Learning Research Conference, College Park, Maryland, Jan. 1979a.

———. The use of biofeedback and related techniques in counseling. Paper presented at the Annual Conference of the Maryland Personnel and Guidance Association, Ocean City, MD, 1979b.

Friedman, M. and R. Rosenman. Type A Behavior and Your Heart. New York: Alfred A. Knopf, 1974.

Gallwey, T. Inner Tennis. New York: Random House, 1976.

Gallwey, T., and B. Kriegel. Inner Skiing. New York: Random House, 1977.

Girdano, Daniel A. "Preventive Treatment—An Intermediate Step," Health Education 8(4): 8-11, 1977.

———. "Performance Based Evaluation," Health Education, 8(2): 13-15, 1977.

Glass, D. C., and J. Singer. Urban Stress. New York: Academic Press, 1972.

Gouldner, A. W. Patterns of Industrial Bureaucracy. Glencoe, Ill.: The Free Press, 1954.

Gunderson, E. K. E., and R. H. Rahe. Life Stress and Illness. Springfield, Ill.: Charles C. Thomas, 1974.

Hopkinson, R. G. and J. B. Collins. The Ergonomics of Lighting. London: MacDonald, 1970.

Jones, R. A. Self-fulfilling Prophecies. Hillsdale, N.J.: L. Erlbaum Associates, 1977.

Kryter, K. The Effects of Noise on Man. New York: Academic Press, 1970.

Layden, M. Escaping the Hostility Trap. Englewood Cliffs, N.J.: Prentice-Hall, 1977.

Levitt, E. E. The Psychology of Anxiety. New York: Bobbs-Merrill, 1967.

Lipowski, Z. J., D. R. Lipsitt, and P. C. Whybrow. Psychosomatic Medicine. New York: Oxford University Press, 1977.

McIntyre, D. A guide to thermal comfort. Applied Ergonomics, 4, (1973), 66–72.

Melton, C. E., et al. Physiological responses in air traffic control personnel: O'Hare Tower. FAA Office of Aviation Medicine, Report No. AM–71-2, 1971.

———. Stress in air traffic personnel: low density towers and flight service stations. FAA Office of Aviation Medicine, Report No. AM–77-23, 1977.

Prevention. Life can be sweeter and longer without sugar. August 1978, 154-162.

Psychology Today. Special report: The new job values. May 1978.

Rosenberg, H. The Book of Vitamin Therapy. Berkeley, Cal.: Berkeley Publishing Corporation, 1974.

Sales, S. Organizational role as a risk factor in coronary disease. Administrative Science Quarterly, 14, (1969), 325–336.

Selye, H. The Stress of Life. New York: McGraw-Hill, 1976.

Thompson, V. A. Modern Organizations. New York: Alfred A. Knopf, 1961.

Toffler, A. Future Shock. New York: Random House, 1971.

Index

A

Adaptation, 10, 17, 107, energy expenditures, 50, 51
Adaptive stress, 50
Adrenal hormone secretion, 15, 52, 89; see also Fight or flight response
Aggression, 56, 58, 89, 90
Alcohol, 95
Anger, 6, 14, 15
Anticipation, 12, 14, 15
Arm and shoulder exercises, 136; arms heavy and warm, 142; back reach, 139-140; extend and reach, 137; flex and pull, 137; relaxing your grip, 142-143; shoulder elevation, 141; shoulder roll, 139; sky reach, 139; wall reach, 138
Arteriosclerosis, 15
Assembly line stress sources, 33, 40
Atherosclerosis, 15
Attitude surveys, 162
Attitudes, 22, 87
Autogenic relaxation, 23, 97, 99
Autonomic nervous system, 22-23

B

Back exercises, 130-133
Behavior patterns, 87
Bennis, W. G., 46
Benson, Herbert, 97
Biking, 159
Biofeedback, 23, 92, 97, 100-104, 112, 164
Biorhythm, 52-53
Boredom, 40-41
Bowling, 160
Breathing, 118-119; diaphragmatic, 120; middle costal, 120; upper costal, 119-120; very deep, 120-121
Breathing exercises: breath counting, 123; breathing down, 121-122; breathing easily, 123-124; controlled tempo breathing, 122-123
Bureaucracy, 46-47

C

Caffeine, 60, 82
Cannon, Walter B., 9

Cardiovascular system, 9, 14-15, 33, 64, 101
Career: counseling and development, 45, 165; lack of guidance, 45, 48
Catecholamine secretion, 52
Change, 17, 50, 54, see also Adaptation
Cholesterol, 15
Circadian rhythms, 52
Collins, J. B., 66
Communications, 47
Competition, 21, 24, 155
Contraction-relaxation exercises, 108-109, 113
Coronary-prone personality, 57
Counseling, 45, 164-165

D

Dancing, 159
Data-gathering methods, 162
Decision-making, 13, 34-36
Delegating responsibilities, 78-79
Dembroski, J. M., 57
Deprivational stress, 40
Diet, 60, 82-95
Digestive system. See Gastrointestinal system
Discrimination, 47-48
Disease, stress caused. See Psychosomatic illness
Distress, 17, 79; signals of, 80-81
Drugs, 95-96

E

Ego involvement, 24, 154; see also Self-concept; self-esteem
Emotional reactivity, 23
Empathy: developing skills, 90-91
Environment. See Office or work environment
Environmental psychology, 163
Eustress, 17, 29, 79
Exercise, 24, 28, 68, 152, 153-154, 165; calisthenics, 160; see also Matrix Relaxation Program
Expectations, 36

F

Facial exercises, 144, 149-150

171

Fight or flight response, 9–10, 23, 151, 152
Follow-up strategies, 79
Freedom posturing exercises, 112
Friedman, Meyer, 33, 57
Frustration, occupational, 44, 48

G

Gallwey, Tim, 155
Galvanic skin response, 57
Gastrointestinal (GI) system, 10, 13–14
General Adaptation Syndrome (GAS), 10
Glass, D. C., 64
Goal directedness, 56
Goal path model, 91
Golf, 160
Gouldner, A. W., 46
Greenwood, James, 4
Gunderson, E. K. E., 50

H

Heart, 14; disease, 3, 15, 33, 57; **see also** Cardiovascular system
High blood pressure. See Hypertension
Holistic stress reduction system, 16, 21–25, 73-74
Homeostasis, 53, 54
Hopkinson, R. G., 66
Hostility, 56, 58, 89–90
Human engineering, 75, 85
Human relations seminars, 165
Humidity, 67
Hurry sickness, 33, 56, 88
Hypertension, 15, 33; essential, 15, 89

I

Infradian rhythms, 52–53
Interruptions and distractions, 79

J

Jet lag syndrome, 53
Job function: altering, 163; ambiguity, 44, 48; boredom, 40–41; complexity, 34; overspecialization, 45–46, 48
Jogging, 158
Jones, R. A., 36

K

Kryter, K., 64

L

Layden, Milton, 89
Leg exercises, 124; gas pedal exercises, 124–126; knee stretch, 127; legs heavy and warm, 128–129; legs loose and light, 129–130; toe raise, 127; toe touch, 127–128
Lifestyle, 20–21
Lighting, 66–67
"Living for the weekend," 41, 48
Lower extremities. See Leg exercises

M

McIntyre, D., 67
Maladaptive coping mechanism, 56
Mantra, 97
Matrix Relaxation Program, 95, 98, 99, 100, 105, 108–112; learning phase, 112; using matrix, 115–118
Medical examination: stress analysis, 162, 165
Meditation, 4, 23, 92, 96, 163
Mental health break, 76
Mood, 80
Muscle tension, 11–12, 105–107; biofeedback, 102; posture, 68
Muscles: shortening of, 109
Muscular system, 6, 10, 11–13; distress signs, 80–81
Music, 164

N

National Institute for Occupational Safety and Health (NIOSH), 40
Neck, head, and face exercises, 145; forced stretch, 146–147; forward, backward neck stretch, 146; head roll, 148; head rotation, 143–144; removing your mask, 149–150; side-to-side neck stretch, 146; your special place, 148–149
Neuromuscular relaxation, 23, 92, 97, 100
Nicotine, 60, 82
Noise, 63–66; decible levels, 65, effects, 66; intensity, 64, 66; responses to, 65; sound frequency, 64
Nutritional engineering, 82–85

O

Occupational stress profile, 29
Office or work environment, 63, 68,

163–164; **see also** Lighting; Noise; Temperature, etc.
Optimal stress level: determining, 79–81
Organizational stress: diagnosis, 161–162; reduction, 161
Organizational Stress Audit (OSA), 24–25, 74, 161, 166
Organizational structure: bureaucracy, 46; communications, 47; reorganization, 52, 163
Overspecialization, 45–46, 48

P

Personal interviews, 162
Personality, 3, 22; Type A, 3, 5, 56–58, 87, 92–93
Personality engineering, 22, 87, 92–93
Physical activity, 23; stress preventive, 153–154; stress reducer, 152–153; **see also** Exercise
Polyphasic behavior, 56, 88
Posture, 68
Premature coronary heart disease (CHD), 57
Process observation, 162
Promotion, 51
Psychological testing, 162
Psychosomatic illness, 10, 19–20, 105, 106, 107; boredom, 40; cardiovascular, 3, 15, 33, 57; gastrointestinal, 13–14; muscular, 11; work overload, 33–34
Pulse: self-regulation, 102

R

Racket sports, 159–160
Rahe, R. H., 50
Recreation, 24, 156
Reiser, Sheldon, 61
Relaxation 95, 101, 111; post-relaxation exercise, 153
Relaxation Response, 163
Relaxation techniques, 91, 107–108; mind direction, 96, preparation for, 113–115
Relaxation training, 22; recall training, 110
Relocation, 51
Reorganization, 52
Residual tension, 111
Respiratory ailments: breathing exercise, 119
Retirement, 53–54
Reverse discrimination, 48
Role conflict, 44
Role switching, 90–91

Rosenberg, Harold, 61
Rosenman, Ray, 33, 57
Running, 158

S

Salt, 61–62, 84
Segmentation, 79
Self-assessment, 29; activity checklist, 156–158; exercise #1 (work overload), 31, 37; exercise #2 (deprivational stress), 39, 42; exercise #3 (organizational frustration), 43, 48; exercise #4 (occupational change), 49, 54; exercise #5 (personality traits), 55, 58
Self-awareness, 101–102, 112
Self-concept, 18; job identity, 45
Self-esteem, 53; hostility and, 89
Selye, Hans, 3, 10, 17, 50, 79, 87, 107
Shiftwork: changes, 52, 53
Shoulder exercises. **See** Arm and shoulder exercises
Singer, J., 64
Skiing, 159
Social engineering, 21–22
Social interactions, 21
Sound: characteristics, 63; **see also** Noise
Stimulants, 60, 82
Stress: analysis, 162; arousal, 111, 152; chronic, 111; costs, 4; factors, 16, 17; quantity, 18, 41, 79; recognizing, 19–20; reduction, 4, 87, 151–152, **see also** Matrix Relaxation Program; response to, 9–10, 18, 22, 23, 111, 151
Stressors, 21; avoiding, 75; organizational, 161
Stretch-relaxation exercises, 109–110, 113
Sugar, 61, 82
"Superman" attitude, 75
Swimming, 159

T

Team building, 163
Technology: changes in, 58
Teeth clenching: exercise, 144
Temperature, 67–68
Tension, **See** Muscle tension
Thompson, Victor, 47
Time: analysis, 77–78; changes, 52–53; management, 77, 88
Time-motion studies, 33
Time urgency, 33, 56, 88
Toffler, Alvin, 50

Total environment approach, 164
Transcendental Meditation, 163
Trunk exercises, 130; arch back, 130–131; back stretch forward, 131–132; back stretch reverse, 132; center of warmth, 133; flat back, 131; standing trunk bend, 133; unlocking your trunk, 134–136

U

Ulcers, 13
Ultradian rhythms, 52
Unitization, 163
Upper extremities. See Arm and shoulder exercises

V

Values, 87
Vasodilation, 110–111
Visceral distress signs, 80
Vitamin deficiency, 61, 82
Vitamins, stress: Recommended Daily Allowance (RDA), 83

W

Walking, 158
Water retention, 62
Weak organ: identification 162–163
Weber, Max, 46
Weight lifting, 160
Work, 22; organization, 78–89; shift changes, 52, 53
Work-By-Objectives (WBO), 75, 88; choosing objectives, 76; planning strategies, 76
Work overload, 32, 75, 80; combination, 32, 35; effects, 37; qualitative, 32, 34; quantitative, 32, 33; self-assessment, 31, 37

X

Xanthines, 60

Y

Yoga, 97; Hatha, 98–99, 109